MW01067726

The Message of the Cross

"BUT GOD FORBID THAT I SHOULD BOAST
EXCEPT IN THE CROSS OF OUR LORD JESUS
CHRIST, BY WHOM THE WORLD HAS BEEN
CRUCIFIED TO ME, AND I TO THE WORLD."
(GALATIANS 6:14 NKJV)

Carl G. Vincent

NEW HARBOR PRESS

RAPID CITY, SD

Vincent/New Harbor Press
1601 Mt Rushmore Rd, Ste 3288
Rapid City, SD 57701
NewHarborPress.com

Ordering Information:
Quantity sales. Special discounts are available on quantity purchases by corporations, associations, and others. For details, contact the "Special Sales Department" at the address above.

The Message of the Cross/Carl G. Vincent. -- 1st ed.

ISBN 978-1-63357-284-3

Contents

This volume is dedicated to the memory
of my dear parents,
Warrington and Lillian Vincent.
They led me to meet Jesus at the cross
when I was twelve years of age.
They continued to love all five of us children
and live as our godly examples
until the day Jesus took them home to glory!

INTRODUCTION

"For the message of the cross is foolishness to those who are perishing, but to us who are being saved it is the power of God." 1 Cor. 1:18

"For the life of the flesh *is* in the blood, and I have given it to you upon the altar to make atonement for your souls; for it *is* the blood *that* makes atonement for the soul."(Leviticus 17:11)

THE MESSAGE OF THE cross is like a rudder on a ship. It doesn't matter how powerful the ship's engines may be or how accurate its navigation system, without a rudder it will not reach its destination. So, it is with the Christian life. It doesn't matter how much education one has or if we fully comprehend the principles of theology, if we do not believe the message of the cross, we will not reach the Biblical destination of victory over sin and a transformed life in Jesus Christ. Since the crucifixion of Jesus Christ, the message of the cross has been and will continue to be the cornerstone of Christianity. The Apostle Paul said, "But God forbid that I should boast except in the cross of our Lord Jesus Christ, by whom the world has been crucified to me, and I to the world."[1] John R. Stott states, "The cross is at the center of evangelical faith."[2]

Since the early church, the cross has been a symbol of Christianity, and the doorway through which we must pass to enter a personal relationship with our Creator and heavenly Father. The Scriptures use several different terms or expressions to describe the crucifixion of Jesus, including His blood, His cross, His suffering, and His death. The cross of Jesus is a historical reality with numerous witnesses seeing Him after His resurrection, even though that reality continues to be denied by some in our postmodern culture.[3]

When we speak of the cross, we are referring to much more than a mere symbol. The cross is often used by Christians as a euphemism expressing the entire redemptive work of Christ. The cross itself is described in Scripture as a "tree."[4] The "cross" or the "tree" cannot save anyone. There were two criminals executed by hanging on crosses the same day Jesus was executed. But they could not save themselves, much less save you and me. So, when we speak of the cross, we are referring to the sacrificial death of Jesus, "the Lamb of God who takes away the sin of the world."[5] The message of the cross includes Jesus' death, burial, resurrection, and ascension. The trials and crucifixion are often referred to as the "passion" of Christ, because of His intense suffering during that Passover season. The message of the cross reveals the good news that Jesus bridges the chasm between sinful man and our holy God and pays the redemptive price

---

1. Gal. 6:14.

2. John R. Stott, *The Cross of Christ* (Downers Grove, IL: InterVarsity Press, 2006), 13.

3. 1 Cor. 15:1-9.

4. Gal. 3:13.

5. John 1:29.

to purchase our passage across that bridge of reconciliation with God. Peter J. Bolt states: "At nine o'clock in the morning on 3 April in the year now known as AD 33, a Jew, Jesus of Nazareth, was put to death on a Roman cross. That event changed the world. Why?"[6] It is the purpose of this book to address and answer, that question.

Jesus giving His life over to the Roman executioners and dying on the cross was not an alternative plan that God devised after mankind sinned. The reality is that the death of Jesus on the cross was accomplished according to the terms of the everlasting covenant,[7] established between the members of the Godhead before the foundation of the world.[8] As Jesus was concluding His earthly ministry and facing His execution, He said, "Now My soul is troubled, and what shall I say? 'Father, save Me from this hour'? But for this purpose, I came to this hour."[9] Great redemptive purposes of God were fulfilled by the crucifixion, resurrection, and ascension of Jesus Christ. For many believers the message of the cross is misunderstood, incomplete or at least confusing because the magnitude of what Jesus accomplished. The message of the cross is multifaceted, originating in eternity past, with ramifications that will not be fully realized until eternity future.

During the fourth century at the councils of Nicaea (325) and Constantinople (381), the Church Fathers hammered out the doctrine of the Trinity. That doctrine has stood the test of time and remains as an insightful theological pillar of our faith. However, the Church

---

6. Peter G. Bolt, *The Cross from a Distance: Atonement in Mark's Gospel*, ed. D. A. Carson, vol. 18, New Studies in Biblical Theology (England; Downers Grove, IL: Apollos; InterVarsity Press, 2004), 13.

7. Heb. 13:20-21.

8. Eph. 1:4.

9. John 12:27.

has never formulated a concise doctrine of the atonement. Ben Witherington III states, "No ecumenical council in Christian history ever established what an orthodox belief about the atonement should and must include or exclude."[10] This book is **not** an attempt to formulate a doctrine of the atonement, but rather an effort to consider the many aspects of our salvation that are contingent upon what Jesus accomplished on our behalf through His death, burial, resurrection, and ascension. So multifaceted, yet complete, is the redemptive ministry of Jesus, that what He accomplished two thousand years ago has impacted every day of history since those events. A. W. Tozer states,

> "We often hear the phrase "the crux of the matter" or "the crux of a situation." The word crux comes from Latin and simply means "cross." Why has the word crux come to be associated with a critical juncture or point in time? Because the cross of Jesus Christ is truly the crux of history. Without the cross, history itself cannot be defined or corrected."[11]

It is through the cross that the mystery of the love of God for all mankind is expressed.[12] In other words, the seed from which the cross of Christ emerges is God's unfathomable love for mankind. The Apostle John wrote, "In this the love of God was manifested toward us, that God has sent His only begotten Son into the world, that we might live through Him."[13] Chapter One addresses the mystery of the

10. Ben Witherington III, *Biblical Theology: The Convergence of the Cannon* (Cambridge, United Kingdom: Cambridge University Press, 2019), 453.

11. A. W. Tozer, *The Radical Cross: Living the Passion of Christ* (Camp Hill, PA: WingSpread, 2005), v.

12. John 3:16.

13. 1 John 4:9.

cross by first discussing the world in which Adam and Eve were created, a world without sin. Then moves to the origin of sin, the nature of sin, and how sin and death have infected all generations since the Garden of Eden. A point to be emphasized is that the God kind of love is first costly. It cost God the extremely expensive gift of His only begotten Son to die on the cross to make possible the reconciliation of sinful mankind back into a personal relationship with Himself. And second, the God kind of love is unconditional, therefore risky, because the cost of love does not guarantee a positive receptivity of that love. It is like paying the high price to express love and then your love is rejected. But rejection does not diminish the value of love. Neither does God love us because we are such good people. God did not wait until we are good to love us--it was while we were yet sinners that God demonstrated His love toward us and Christ died for us.[14] George Eldon Ladd says, "For Paul the most ignominious and cruel form of human execution has become the place where God supremely displayed His love."[15]

The cross was in the heart of God even before the days of creation. Scriptures reveal that Jesus was "the Lamb slain from the foundation of the world."[16] The Old Testament foreshadows the message of the cross as discussed in chapter two. In chapter three we turn our attention to the cost of the cross as it is revealed in the ceremonial sacrifices on the Day of Atonement and the sacrifice of Jesus to inaugurate the New Covenant. The lessons taught through the ceremonies on the Day of Atonement[17] provide a pattern that helps

14. Rom. 5:8.

15. George Eldon Ladd, *A Theology of the New Testament*, rev. ed. (Grand Rapids, MI: William B. Eerdmans Publishing Company, 1993) 465.

16. Rev. 13:8.

17. Lev. 16:1-34.

us understand what Jesus as the Mediator of the New Covenant accomplished through His death, burial, resurrection, and ascension. First, the Day of Atonement and the cross of Jesus, are acts of God's grace that reveal the magnitude of God's love. Our heavenly Father was willing to pay the scandalous price in making every provision for His sinful children to be cleansed of sin and reconciled with Him. Second, after all the provisions that God in His grace has provided, reconciliation with God further requires that sinful man personally take steps of faith to experience forgiveness and reconciliation with God. Third, being reconciled with God is a life transformational experience whereby sinners are transformed from the place of slavery to sin into a place of rest in the Lord. And finally, being reconciled with God firmly establishes the hope of glory in the heart of every believer in Jesus Christ, and the hope of glory transcends all the riches and pleasures this world has to offer. A further and helpful comment about "atonement" is made by D. Brockway,

> Atonement is one of the few theological terms with roots in the English language. It is the process by which two (typically estranged) parties are made "at-one" with each other. The Old Testament usually mentions atonement in the context of worship, primarily in reference to temple sacrifices. The word does not occur in the New Testament, but the concept is implied throughout—particularly in the metaphoric imagery used to describe the saving work of Christ.[18]

18. D. Brockway, "Atonement," ed. John D. Barry et al., *The Lexham Bible Dictionary* (Bellingham, WA: Lexham Press, 2016).

So manifold are the accomplishments of Jesus through His death, burial, resurrection, and ascension that make our salvation possible, that this author has categorized those accomplishments under four different aspects of salvation as shown in the chart below:

Jesus Christ the Son of God

Mediator of the New Covenant

The Cross and the Atonement

Acts of Grace	Steps of Faith	Places of Rest	Hope of Glory
Chosen/Predestined	Conviction/Repentance	Covenant	Immortality
Propitiation/Expiation	Justified/Righteous	Peace/Joy	Inheritance
Book of Life/Hope	Forgiven/Reconciled/United	Access/Vision	Reign w/Christ
Redemption/Ransom	Regeneration/Sealed	Adoption	Glorious Light
Calling/Deliverance	Power/Authority	Liberty	New Jerusalem

Without Jesus Christ crucified, buried, resurrected, and ascended, there would be no salvation for sinners, because it is impossible for sinful man to save himself. But Jesus Christ who was both God and man, stood in the gap between God and man as the Mediator of the New Covenant, through which He made atonement for sinners. Now, through Jesus Christ as our Mediator we can be reconciled with our Creator and heavenly Father. There are two aspects to the concept of atonement: first, the process of cleansing or purifying, and second, the process of reconciliation. Notice that both purification and reconciliation require a process to reach the consummation of our salvation. Therefore, this author explains the origin, purification, reconciliation, and consummation of our salvation by separating these processes into four categories as outlined in the chart above.

The "Acts of Grace" were performed by God without any input from mankind. God performed some of these acts even before the foundation of the world. These acts of grace reveal that long before we did either good or evil, God loved us and committed Himself by covenant to perform these dimensions of His grace for our salvation. These acts of grace are discussed in chapter four.

The second aspect of our salvation includes "Steps of Faith" which are discussed in chapter five. Steps of faith require and demand the believer's participation with God by faith to experience His benefits.[19] The third aspect focuses on "Places of Rest." God's plan of salvation includes places of rest for every believe, and these are discussed in chapter six. And final aspect of what Jesus has accomplished for us through His death, burial, resurrection, and ascension is the "Hope of Glory", which serves as an anchor of our soul as we persevere through the challenges of living an overcoming life in the here and now. The hope of glory is discussed in chapter seven. All these aspects of salvation should be operational in each believer's life simultaneously. It is the author's objective to assist believers in understanding more comprehensively these aspects of our salvation and contribute to a fuller understanding of the multifaceted aspects of what Jesus accomplished through the cross. The ultimate purpose is to encourage every believer to apply these aspects of the message of the cross to their personal experience as we strive to grow into the "fullness of the stature of Christ."[20]

Chapter eight concludes our discussions on the message of the cross by challenging each of us to not only rejoice in what Jesus has done for us through His death burial, resurrection, and ascension,

---

19. Rom. 1:17.
20. Eph. 4:13.

but to fulfill the words of Jesus when "He said to *them* all, 'If anyone desires to come after Me, let him deny himself, and take up his cross daily, and follow Me.'"[21] To believe on Jesus Christ the risen Savior and follow Him is the means for gaining eternal life and the grounds for the hope of ruling and reigning with the Lord Jesus in glory forever! For "God was in Christ reconciling the world to Himself, not imputing their trespasses to them, and has committed to us the word of reconciliation."[22]

As we move through the pages ahead it is this author's prayer that the Holy Spirit will bring you clarity of understanding and increase your redemptive wisdom and faith regarding the message of the cross. There are two intended personal applications for the understanding of the message of the cross that you will hopefully gain through the following pages: First, it is intended that you will better grasp the complex wisdom of the cross and apply those realities to your personal experience. The danger that every Christian must guard against while seeking to understand the message of the cross, is that one may substitute the "wisdom of words" for the personal experience of the cross, which can make the message of the cross of no effect.[23] Second, in gaining a better understanding of what Jesus accomplished through the cross will enable us to participate more fully in the transformational power of the cross. In other words, if the rulers of this age had known the hidden wisdom in the cross, "they would not have crucified the Lord of glory."[24] The value of godly wisdom revealed in the message of the cross makes many earthly things we have treasured become what the Apostle Paul describes

21. Luke 9:23.
22. 2 Cor. 5:19.
23. 1 Cor. 1:17.
24. 1 Cor. 2:7-8.

as "rubbish" or "dung".[25] To experience the cross of Christ is to experience a transformation of our life and personal values, which in turn will impact the stewardship of our time, talent, resources, and relationships.

25. Phil. 3:8.

The Mystery of the Cross

"To me, who am less than the least of all the saints, this grace was given, that I should preach among the Gentiles the unsearchable riches of Christ, and to make all see what *is* the fellowship of the mystery, which from the beginning of the ages has been hidden in God who created all things through Jesus Christ" (Eph. 3:8-9)

OVER THE YEARS YOU have experienced members of your family or friends having their lives cut short. It is always painful to experience the death of a loved one because death interrupts our relationships, crushing our dreams, hopes, and plans that give our lives purpose. Recently I ministered at the memorial service for my brother who was thirteen years younger than me. A little over thirty-five years earlier I ministered at the memorial service for his infant daughter. The point is that death is no respecter of persons, and no one is exempt.

The death of a family member or friend leaves us in the pain of grief. We find ourselves in tears and at a loss as to how to get ourselves reoriented. We feel alone and empty. We ask why? Why did this have to happen? Why did this have to happen now? Why didn't

God intervene and prevent this loss? Some become angry with God as if death was His fault. In our grief, reason becomes blurred, and life and death seem scrambled into a painful mystery. We try to read the Bible, but can we find comfort there when we think of Jesus who never did anything wrong, yet He was condemned by His own countrymen and hung on a cross by Roman soldiers. It sure seems confusing. Are there any answers to this mystery of life and death?

The realities that guide our understanding into resolution of our confusion and grief are discovered through the unveiling of the mystery of the cross. This mystery continues to be a source of controversy and contention in theological and academic communities. Nevertheless, the Apostle Paul states, "the message of the cross is foolishness to those who are perishing, but to us who are being saved it is the power of God."[26]

A World Without Sin and Death:

Insight and understanding into the mystery of the cross is gained through faith in our resurrected Savior Jesus Christ. Faith that gives us the victory over death has two primary sources: The first and primary source of faith is derived from the reality that Jesus died on the cross, was buried, but on the third day He arose from the dead, disarming principalities and powers making a public spectacle of them, triumphing over them.[27] Our resurrected Lord Himself said, "I *am* He who lives, and was dead, and behold, I am alive forevermore. Amen. And I have the keys of Hades and of Death."[28] "Keys" in Scripture speak figuratively of authority, and Jesus Christ has authority over

26. 1 Cor. 1:18.
27. Col. 2:15.
28. Rev. 1:18.

sin, death, and the grave. Therefore, through faith in Jesus Christ, believers are delivered from the fear and bondage of death.[29] The second source of faith that guides us to victory over death and releases insight and understanding regarding the mystery of the cross comes through the person and work of the Holy Spirit. Jesus said,

> "When He, the Spirit of truth, has come, He will guide you into all truth; for He will not speak on His own *authority*, but whatever He hears He will speak; and He will tell you things to come. He will glorify Me, for He will take of what is Mine and declare *it* to you."[30]

The ministry of the Holy Spirit was neglected by the Church for many centuries. Even since the Reformation He has been overlooked by much of the church community in favor of the enlightening of the modern mind by so called science. Although science has proven to have no solution for the bondage of sin and death. However, God in His wisdom has a solution, and has sent the Holy Spirit to reveal His wisdom to us. During the 20th century God graciously released a tremendous refreshing presence of the Holy Spirit. That century has been designated as, "The Century of the Holy Spirit."[31] The Holy Spirit is not some mystical superstitious ghost of the dark ages. He is the member of the Godhead that dwells in the heart of every believer. He is the "Holy Spirit of promise" who quickens faith, guiding

---

29. Heb. 2:14-15.
30. John 16:13-14.
31. Vinson Synan, *The Century of the Holy Spirit: 100 Years of Pentecostal and Charismatic Renewal* (Nashville, TE: Thomas Nelson Publishers, 2001), ix.

believers into all truth by releasing heaven's wisdom and revelation,[32] making it possible for each of us to understand the mystery of the cross and empowers each of us to live victoriously over sin and death.

A Biblical mystery is not something absurd or a fantasy. A Biblical mystery is a divine secret or a reality in the purposes and plans of God that has not been revealed or unveiled. Spiros Zodhiates defines a Biblical "mystery" as "some sacred thing hidden or secret which is naturally unknown to human reason and is only known by the revelation of God."[33] The message of the cross remains an incomprehensible mystery to the natural man. "But God has revealed them (*mysteries or the hidden wisdom of God*) to us through His Spirit. For the Spirit searches all things, yes, the deep things of God" (emphasis mine).[34] Hence, the Holy Spirit wants to grant each of us insight and revelation regarding divine mysteries. "Now we have received, not the spirit of the world, but the Spirit who is from God, that we might know the things that have been freely given to us by God."[35] Therefore, ask and expect the Holy Spirit to reveal the mystery of the cross to you.

Through faith in our resurrected Lord and the help of the Holy Spirit we will grasp the meaning of death as unveiled and defined in the mystery of the cross. Death is separation/alienation from God, the source of life. There is a tendency within our culture to consider life as only a biological phenomenon. But "life" has its source beyond the limits of biology, originating in God, who alone is the giver and sustainer of life. Remember when God created Adam, he was first an inanimate lifeless lump of clay until God "breathed into his nostrils

---

32. Eph. 1:14-17.

33. Spiros Zodhiates, *The Complete Word Study Dictionary: New Testament* (Chattanooga, TN: AMG Publishers, 2000).

34. 1 Cor. 2:10.

35. 1 Cor. 2:12.

the breath of life; and he became a living being."[36] God breathed His own life into Adam's body and God's life is eternal. The Creation narrative has absolutely nothing to say up to this point about death. In other words, the first mention of death appears after God placed Adam in the Garden of Eden to tend it and keep it.[37] Then God commanded Adam saying, "Of every tree of the garden you may freely eat; but of the tree of the knowledge of good and evil you shall not eat, for in the day that you eat of it you shall surely die."[38] The creation narrative continues with God taking a rib from Adam's side and making a woman, a helper comparable to him.[39]

The Origin of Sin and Death:

Suddenly chapter three of Genesis opens with a being described as "the serpent"[40] that talked with Eve. The serpent questioned her about God's command and prohibition regarding eating of the fruit from the tree of the knowledge of good and evil. The serpent was so subtle in his conversation with Eve that he deceived her, and she ate the forbidden fruit. She then gave it to Adam, and he willfully ate the fruit from the tree of the knowledge of good and evil.

After Adam and Eve ate of that which God had forbidden, they experienced three consequences for their disobedience: (1) Their physical nature changed. Their eyes were opened, and they realized they were naked.[41] They were no longer clothed with the glory of God and innocence, but shrouded in fear, guilt, and shame. (2) Their

---

36. Gen. 2:7
37. Gen. 2:15.
38. Gen. 2:16-17.
39. Gen. 2:20-25.
40. Gen. 3:1-4.
41. Gen. 3:7.

relationship with God changed. They first tried to hide their nakedness with fig leaves and being afraid, even tried to hide from God. But God soon confronted them, and they were subsequently driven out of the Garden. Now, separated from the manifest presence of God, they were experiencing spiritual death, and began the process of dying physically. (3) Their relationship with all nature changed. Now Eve would experience pain in childbirth and her husband would rule over her. God cursed the ground, so Adam would have to till the soil by the sweat of his brow, laboring not only against thorns and thistles,[42] but the whole of creation over which they had been given dominion was now under the bondage of corruption.

Before we move forward in the Biblical narrative, consider more carefully the trauma Adam must have experienced by having disobeyed God and then with a guilty conscience having to stand before Him. I recently heard about a nurse in our local hospital who inadvertently gave a patient too large of a dose of medicine. Then she had to go and face her supervisor and confess her mistake and apologize. Fortunately, the large dose of medicine did not harm the patient, but it was a traumatic and tearful experience for that nurse. It is hard for us to imagine the gravity of the meeting between God and Adam.

Adam and Eve being afraid and trying to hide themselves from God, may seem on the surface as a lack of faith or even childishness. But think of the seriousness with which God may have conversed with them. God is not a man; He is God Almighty. In heaven the angels cry holy, holy, holy, before Him day and night! God had spoken the world into existence and more recently created Eve to be a helpmeet for Adam. These are events that would make any human being seem exceedingly insignificant in the presence of God, even if he

42. Gen. 3:16-19; Rom. 8:20-22.

were not guilty. Consider what it was like when God came down on Mt. Sinai to speak to the Children of Israel. Upon hearing God's voice, the Children were so scared that they did not want to talk to God, and Moses himself said, "I am exceedingly afraid and trembling."[43] In view of God's holiness, it was a miracle of divine mercy that God did not destroy Adam and Eve on the spot! They had disobeyed God and offended His holiness. It seems to be a wonder that Adam didn't simply collapse and die. Think about what happened to Ananias and Saphira.[44] However, guilty Adam did face God, and then went on to pyhsically live over nine hundred years, but I am certain he never, ever forgot that day.

There are three practical insights we gain from Adam's experience so far. First, even though God created mankind in His image and likeness, man was created fallible. Second, it is not discussed in the creation narrative, but the reality is that man was created with a conscience that serves to guide him in decisions of right and wrong. We know that Adam's conscience was functioning because he experienced fear and guilt after his disobedience. However, man can willfully override the voice of his conscience. "Therefore, *you* must be subject (*to God appointed authorities*), not only because of wrath, but also for conscience' sake"[45] (emphasis mine). And third, Adam's sin of disobedience introduced sin into this world.[46] But God already had a plan of atonement to resolve sin and cover his nakedness.[47] As we continue, we will bring greater clarity to the divine wisdom

---

43. Heb. 12:18-21; Exod. 20:18-26.
44. Acts 5:1-11.
45. Rom. 13:5.
46. Rom. 5:12-14.
47. Rom. 5:18-21.

contained in the atonement. But for now, we can proceed with this assurance that sin and death do not have the last word, God does!

Beyond the consequences to be suffered by Adam and Eve because of their disobedience, it is also helpful to consider the consequences of God's curse upon the serpent. The Lord God said to the serpent,

> "Because you have done this, you *are* cursed more than all cattle, and more than every beast of the field; On your belly you shall go, and you shall eat dust all the days of your life. And I will put enmity between you and the woman, and between your seed and her Seed; He shall bruise your head, and you shall bruise His heel."[48]

We are uncertain of the exact nature of this subtle creature called "the serpent." But in the Book of the Revelation this creature is referred to as the great dragon, that serpent of old, called the Devil and Satan, who deceives the whole world.[49] From God's response to the serpent we gain two insights into the mystery of the cross: First, God placed a curse upon the serpent and continued by saying that He would put enmity between the serpent and the woman, between the serpent's seed and the woman's seed. That enmity continues to sustain an ongoing conflict between the seed of the serpent and the seed of the woman until this present time. But the greatest manifestation of this conflict is the enmity the religious leaders hurled against Jesus Christ who was holy, harmless, undefiled, and separate from sinners, yet because of their envy they crucified Him.[50] Second,

48. Gen. 3:14-15.
49. Rev. 12:9a.
50. Mark 15:10.

the seed of the woman will bruise the head of the serpent and the serpent will bruise the heel of the seed of the woman. This is considered by many scholars as a great promise and a prophecy that foresees the victory of Jesus over the devil. Henry M. Morris states, "the prophecy looks forward to the time when Satan will be completely crushed beneath the feet of the woman's triumph seed."[51] Jesus disarmed Satan through His death on the cross and resurrection from the dead. The ultimate victory will be when Jesus returns and "the kingdoms of this world become the kingdoms of our Lord and His Christ, and he shall reign forever and ever."[52] Following Jesus' reign on the earth for one thousand years the devil and his cohorts will be cast into the lake of fire. That will consummate the conflict between the seed of the serpent and the seed of the woman. It will end the earthly presence of the serpent, the devil, and evil forever!

According to the details in Genesis chapter three, the "serpent" tempted Eve. Think about how this could have been an altogether different kind of an encounter. He could have exhorted her to be content and celebrate her fellowship with God and enjoy the beauty and fruitfulness of her present environment. Rather, he tempted her to be discontent, to eat what was forbidden, seek to be like God, and to know good and evil. That was because the "serpent" was speaking on behalf of the "evil one," the "devil". The devil is a pernicious liar, murderer, and destroyer. There is no truth in him.[53] His motivation is power for the sake of control over others, as opposed to power for the sake of blessing and prospering others. The evil one has no capacity to be constructive or bless others if he cannot control them. In other

51. Henry M. Morris, *The Genesis Record: A Scientific & Devotional Commentary on the Book of Beginnings* (Grand Rapids, MI: Baker Book House, 1976), 120.

52. Rev. 11:15b.

53. John 8:44.

words, the devil gives to get. He maintains a defensive posture with the compulsion to destroy whatever someone else has labored to construct. We learn from history that devilish men like Herod the Great even killed his own family members when he considered they were opposing him or his purposes.

Understanding the mystery of the cross is contingent upon knowing and believing the truth. The truth is that God is the sovereign Creator of mankind and God is love.[54] God does not force anyone to love Him. The God kind of love must be expressed freely and without coercion. The test of love is obedience and obedience must be learned. Even Jesus had to "learn obedience."[55] In His toughest test of obedience He said, "Not My will but Your will be done."[56] Jesus said, "If you love Me, keep My commandments."[57] God as the sovereign Creator of mankind, gives commands to guide man's character development. God did not create mankind to be robots programed to do His bidding. Rather, He created sons and daughters in His image with the capacity to make moral decisions and serve as stewards over this earth. Therefore, every person is free to choose to love God or reject God. However, every person is also responsible and accountable to God their Creator for all their words and actions.[58] Adam and Eve were created innocent, but responsible and accountable before God for their personal words and actions.

Eve was deceived by the serpent, but Adam willfully disobeyed God. Adam's disobedience inflicted his posterity and the world over

---

54. 1 John 4:8.
55. Heb. 5:8.
56. Matt. 26:39; Mark 14:36; Luke 22:42.
57. John 14:15, 15:10.
58. Matt. 12:36; Rom. 14:12; Heb. 4:13.

which he had been given dominion with sin and death.[59] God did not create sin nor death. On the other hand, Adam is the source of sin and death. Adam was responsible and accountable to God his Creator for the stewardship which God had granted him. However, when Adam disobeyed God's command, the purpose of God to have a royal family of sons and daughters was not lost. In God's wisdom and great love for mankind, He had already made provision in eternity past for mankind's victory over sin and death through the atonement! The atonement of the Old Testament only covered sin as it looked forward through the eyes of faith to the cross of Christ where His shed blood completely washes away our sin to be remembered no more. It is sufficient for now to say that the purpose of the atonement is the forgiveness of sins and thus making reconciliation with the Father is made possible.

Adam's disobedience was a violation of God's command, an offense against His holiness. Disobedience and defiance are the substance of sin, and the wages or consequences of sin is death.[60] The word "moral" means: "of or relating to principles of right and wrong in behavior."[61] Adam knew that it was wrong to eat what God had clearly forbidden. John H. Walton declares,

> The most vile aspect of human sin is not what it did to each of us but what it did to God. Our sin is a desecration of God. This desecration does not alter who God is, but it dishonors Him. It can be compared to the disrespect done to a country when its flag

---

59. Rom. 5:12-19.
60. Rom.6:23.
61. Merriam-Webster, *Merriam-Webster's Collegiate Dictionary* (Springfield, MA: Merriam-Webster, 1996).

is trampled on, torn, smeared with excrement, or burned. The country does not suffer in the process, but a patriot will jump to its defense, nonetheless. In a similar vein, the most lamentable result of sin to an Israelite is not that it makes people bad, but that it makes God distant.[62]

Right and wrong are consequential issues for every person and society. Morals have intrinsic values because they guide our behavior into an alignment with the nature of God. Because God is the sovereign Creator of mankind His moral laws are binding upon every person, whether they believe in God or not. God gives every person freedom of choice, but every person will stand accountable to God on Judgment Day for the choices they made. Without the constraint of godly morals, this life becomes meaningless. Francis Schaeffer states,

> Modern people, on their basis of reason, see themselves only as machines. But as they move into the area of non-reason and look for optimism, they find themselves separated from reason and without any human or moral values.... There is no certainty, **no categories upon which to distinguish between reality and illusion.**[63] (Emphasis mine).

---

62. John H. Walton, *Genesis: The NIV Application Commentary* (Grand Rapids, MI: Zondervan, 2001), 231.

63. Francis A. Schaeffer, *How Shall We Then Live? The Rise and Decline of Western Thought and Culture* (Old Tappan, NJ: Fleming H. Revell Company, 1976), 202.

The experience of Adam teaches us that when anyone chooses to disobey God in favor of doing whatever they personally want to do, sin and chaos will result. God has given His laws and the Holy Spirit has been poured out for the purpose of guiding each person's conscience and establishing the boundaries for moral conduct. Francis J. Beckwith affirms this by stating, "There exist an eternally self-existing moral agent named God, who created the universe *ex nihilo*. The universe is completely and absolutely contingent upon God for its beginning as well its existence."[64] J. P. Moreland and William Lane Craig state, "One ought to be moral because moral law is true and is constituted by the non-arbitrary commands of a good, just, wise, loving God or because the **moral law is grounded in the way we are designed by such a God to function properly**.[65] (Emphasis mine). Sam Storms states,

> That which distinguishes man from the animal kingdom is the *imago Dei*, the image of God; the image of God has traditionally been identified with such things as rationality, self-consciousness, the exercise of dominion, and moral conscience; however, we must be careful in defining the image of God in wholly functional terms. **The image of God is as much a** state **as it is a** capacity. The image is not to be conceived as an end in a process whereby an unborn entity progresses into personhood. The im-

64. Beckwith, Francis J., William Lane Craig, and J. P. Moreland, eds., *To Everyone An Answer: A Case for the Christian Worldview,* (Downers Grove, IL: InterVarsity Press, 2004), 14.

65. J. P. Moreland and William Lane Craig, *Philosophical Foundations for a Christian Worldview* (Downers Grove, IL: InterVarsity Press, 2003), 404.

age is a given, not a goal to which the fetus moves in its physiological development. No one denies that the fetus develops. But this development is not from non-person to part-person to full-person, but rather from full-person to the consummate expression and experience of all that personhood entails.[66] (Emphasis mine).

Mankind did not evolve from some lower form of being into his present state. No! Mankind was created in the image and likeness of our sovereign Creator God. Because God is our sovereign Creator, Adam had to stand before God to give an account for his actions; just as every person will have to stand before God to give an account for his or her life on judgement day. Some people want to be free from accountability to God, but that is an impossibility. All of us want to be free, but freedom does not exclude our accountability before God. Never! The words of Jesus make it clear that hell is not characterized by freedom as some may think.[67] Hell is a prison or place of confinement to an eternity of darkness and weeping in torment for all those who have rejected God's gift of salvation.[68] The pathway to true freedom and blessings is living in harmony with the will of God, and not doing whatever I want to do. Adam lost his place in paradise and his personal freedom when he chose to do what he wanted rather than obeying God.

Although God created man in His own image and likeness, man is not God. It was the serpent that told Eve that if she ate the forbidden

---

66. Sam Storms, *Christian Ethics* (Oklahoma City, OK: Sam Storms, 2006), 7.
67. Matt. 8:12.
68. Matt. 13:41-42; Luke 12:5; Mark 9:44.

fruit she would be like God.[69] She was already like God, created in His image and simply needed time to experience life with God which would saturate her with divine wisdom. But the serpent tempted her to take a short cut to instantly maximize her birthright. Adam took the matter into his own hands and in his foolish disobedience plunged himself and his posterity into life on earth under the oppression of an evil task master. Thereby, he forfeited his stewardship of dominion over the earth. Now the whole world "lies under the sway of the evil one."[70] However, rather than completely destroying mankind, God in His mercy provided a substitutionary sacrifice for Adam's sin by killing an animal. This made an atonement for him through the shedding of innocent blood until the fullness of time when God's own Son would pay the full price for Adam's redemption. The mystery of the cross includes an atonement for sin through a substitutionary sacrifice, looking forward to the day when the woman's seed would bruise the head of the serpent.[71]

Adam and Eve began experiencing life outside paradise. Their biological existence continued until each of them eventually died physically. D. A. Carson states, "... sin establishes the plotline of the Bible."[72] The Apostle Paul writes, "Just as through one man (*Adam*) sin entered the world, and death through sin, and thus death spread to all men, because all sinned."[73] (Emphasis mine). Death is completely contrary and opposite to God's nature. God is life and it is impossible

---

69. Gen. 3:5.

70. 1 John 5:19.

71. Gen. 3:15.

72. D. A. Carson, "Sin's Contemporary Significance," in *Fallen: A Theology of Sin*, ed. Christopher W. Morgan and Robert A. Peterson, Theology in Community (Wheaton, IL: Crossway, 2013), 22.

73. Rom. 5:12.

for God to sin. He cannot die or lie or change.[74] Adam introduced sin into God's created order, thereby introducing death and disorder. Sin has the insidious nature of evil that infects both body and soul releasing a disposition of defiance against God. This disposition of defiance is expressed by our propensity to sin, thus our "sinful nature."

All of us inherit our sinful nature from our parents going back to Adam and Eve, the original parents. Keep in mind that as parents you do not need to teach your children to rebel or cheat or steal, because they commit sins according to the impulse of their sinful nature. Therefore, a sober examination of the events in the first three chapters of Genesis reveal three realities: (1) All of us are included in the "seed of the woman" and will never be at peace with the "seed of the serpent." So, do not spend your efforts in trying to be at peace with them. Instead seek to be at peace with God through His redemptive provisions made at the cross. (2) As a result of sin, all mankind has an appointment with death and judgment. Hence, prepare now to meet God for today is a day of salvation. (3) All of us are born sinners and sin wars in our members. Therefore, to gain the victory over sin and death one must believe on the Lord Jesus, repent of personal sin, be buried in baptismal waters, and be born again by receiving the Holy Spirit into one's heart.[75]

It was not until after the death, burial, resurrection, and asension of Jesus Christ that God's ultimate solution to sin and death was clearly manifest. From the days of Adam until the crucifixion of Jesus, God revealed His plan of salvation through types and shadows pointing towards His Son, Jesus, the "Lamb of God who takes away

---

74. Num. 23:19; Mal. 3:6; Heb. 13:8; Titus 1:2.
75. John 3:3-7.

THE MESSAGE OF THE CROSS

the sin of the world."[76] And you were "chosen in Him before the foundation of the world."[77] In spite of the offenses you caused and/or experienced as a result of sin, we have hope beyond sin and death. God has a great plan for you in this life and unspeakable glory in the life to come! That is what the message of the cross is all about. However, do not get the message of the cross confused with dead religion which cannot comprehend the message of the cross.

The Nature of Sin:

In the following pages the term "sin" will be used as a generic term that includes numerous categories of attitudes and actions. The four broadest expressions or categories of sin include: (1) Rebellion – The willful and continual refusal to obey a recognized authority including a stance of defiant contention. When a police officer signals for a person to stop and that person not only refuses to stop but continues their action with the attitude or words; "Don't tell me what to do." That is rebellion. (2) Transgression – The willful violation of a stated law. If the sign says, "Keep off the grass," and you willfully walk on the grass, that is a transgression. (3) Iniquity – That distorted, twisted, or perverted manner which sin causes all people to see God and others incorrectly, like a camera out of focus giving a distorted view of an image. Even though the image is not distorted, the camera out of focus will make it appear distorted. That is how iniquity works in our life—we see God and others in a distorted manner. (4) Evil – That insidious corruption that destroys until nothing remains, like tooth decay. If the decay is not ground out of the tooth, it will continue

---

76. John 1:26.
77. Eph. 1:4; Rev. 13:8.

until there is neither decay nor a tooth. Evil weakens or destroys all it meets rather than strengthening and constructing. The devil is the original "the evil one."[78] J. Rodman Williams states, "Sin inevitably points to the irrational and is the utter antithesis of order and good sense."[79] John Murry adds, "Sin is the contradiction of the perfection of God, and He cannot but recoil against that which is the contradiction of Himself. Such recoil is His holy indignation.... (Rom. 1:18). The judgment of God upon sin is essentially His wrath."[80]

Sin and death are negatives in the message of the cross. We will address the positives in the chapters ahead. Until we understand the origin, presence, and destructive nature of sin we will not comprehend the mystery of the cross. From the third chapter of Genesis throughout the remaining chapters of the Bible, all individuals are born sinners. People do not sin and thus become sinners. NO! Every person inherits a sin nature from his or her parents and as a result they each sin. Throughout the ages God has been progressively and sequentially revealing His plan to rescue man from sin, including its penalty, power, and presence. Man is incapable of delivering himself from sin and death. God is the only One capable of resolving sin and giving us the hope of a future without sin and death![81] In other words, God does not simply overlook sin. No! The wages of sin is death and those wages must be paid! And in the fullness of time God Himself paid man's sin debt at the cross. The emphasis so far in this chapter is focused upon the mystery of the cross. The unveiling of that mystery

78. John17:15; Eze. 28:14-15.

79. J. Rodman Williams, *Renewal Theology: Systematic Theology from a Charismatic Perspective*, 3 vol. in one; vol. 1, (Grand Rapids, MI: Zondervan, 1996), 223.

80. John Murray, *Redemption Accomplished and Applied* (Grand Rapids, MI: William B. Eerdmans, 2015), 28.

81. Rev. 21:4.

requires that we understand the origins of sin and death. The first three chapters of Genesis reveal these origins, but this is only the beginning of the story.

God expressed His wisdom and redemptive mercy to Adam and Eve by providing skins to cover their nakedness.[82] Even though the Scripture does not state this explicitly, it is implied that Adam and Eve witnessed the shedding of blood of an innocent animal necessary for God to make coverings for them. This illustrates the reality that sin is a moral violation of man's relationship with God, thereby incurring the just penalty of death.[83] God is just, therefore He must judge those who commit sin. God also loves all mankind. Therefore, He devised a plan of salvation before the foundation of the world to deliver mankind from sin. Arthur W. Pink states,

> God dealt with Adam and Eve in mercy, but in doing so He first met the claims of His broken law. In clothing them with skins God showed them by forceful symbol that sin could only be covered atone for, for the Hebrew word for atone means to cover at the cost of sacrifice, by life being taken, by blood being shed. And so in Eden itself we find the first type and foreshadowing of the cross of Christ.[84]

Sin now separated Adam and Eve from the manifest presence of God and the intimate fellowship they had enjoyed; the shedding of blood atoned for their sin and prevented their complete annihilation. John Walton states, "The overwhelming loss was not paradise, it

82. Gen. 3:21.
83. Gen. 2:17; Rom. 6:23
84. Arthur W. Pink, *Gleanings in Genesis* (Chicago, IL: Moody Press1975), 64.

was God. Throughout all of the rest of the Old Testament one never hears talk of regaining the comfort of Eden, but regaining access to God's presence was paramount."[85] After Adam's exposition from the Garden of Eden access to God was through prayer and the offering of sacrifices. From the time of Adam until the outpouring of the Holy Spirit on the Day of Pentecost a relationship with God for most people was like participating in a relationship at a distance, rather than the intimate relationship Adam enjoyed with God before sin.

Man was created to center his life in God, cooperating harmoniously in accomplishing His will in the earth realm. Originally Adam had enjoyed that kind of life having intimate fellowship with God in an ordered environment that flowed together in harmony, beauty, and fruitfulness. When he disobeyed God, he not only introduced sin and death into the world, but sin disrupted God's good order bringing disorder. John H. Walton states. "Disorder is the result of sin, and it continues to reflect our inability to be as good as we were designed to be.... Sin has made us low-functioning creatures...."[86] Not only mankind, but also nature itself groans and labors under the frustration of corruption and disorder.[87]

Sin and Death Infect the Generations:

Not only did Adam and Eve sin, but they passed their "sin nature" on to their children. Now outside of the Garden of Eden, access to God was no longer a passive experience as it had been in the Garden of Eden. Now a relationship with God demanded faith. Cain and Abel

---

85. Walton, *Genesis: The NIV Application Commentary*, 231.
86. John. H. Walton, *The Lost World of Adam and Eve* (Downers Grove, IL: InterVarsity Press, 2015), 151.
87. Rom. 8:22.

in the "process of time" came to bring offerings to the Lord. The place where the offerings were presented is not stated. They were probably presented at the east of the Garden of Eden where the cherubim with the flaming sword were standing guard.[88] There has been much discussion regarding the two offerings, but for our purposes it is sufficient to note that it was "by faith Abel offered to God a more excellent sacrifice than Cain."[89]

The point is that God respected Abel's offering and did not respect Cain's.[90] As a result Cain became very angry and his countenance fell. "So, the LORD said to Cain, 'Why are you angry? And why has your countenance fallen? If you do well, will you not be accepted? And if you do not do well, sin lies at the door. And its desire *is* for you, but you should rule over it.'"[91] Cain refused to humble himself and offer an acceptable sacrifice. Therefore, he allowed sin to rule over him and it came to pass that he killed his brother Abel.[92] This is evidence of the "enmity" that God said would exist between the seed of the serpent and the seed of the woman.

Both Cain and Abel were the seed of the woman, but Cain refused to humble himself and meet the faith requirements necessary for a relationship with God. He thereby willfully gave himself over to an agreement with the seed of the serpent, thus aligning himself with the "evil one" who was a murderer from the beginning.[93] The Scripture says, "No one can serve two masters; for either he will hate the one and love the other, or else he will be loyal to one and despise

---

88. Gen. 3:24.
89. Heb. 11:4.
90. Gen. 4:4-5
91. Gen. 4:6-7.
92. Gen. 5:8.
93. John 8:44.

the other."[94] You can easily see that the battle lines were formed. The conflict gained momentum through the years until wickedness was so great that "the Lord was sorry that He had made man on the earth."[95]

Genesis chapter four concludes with an account of the birth of Seth through whom the Messiah would eventually come. From the birth of Seth until the flood in the days of Noah there were men of faith. For example, the Scripture states, "By faith Enoch was taken away so that he did not see death, *'and was not found, because God had taken him'; for* before he was taken, he had this testimony, that he pleased God."[96] However there are two factors that we need to consider. First, even though there were men who "called on the name of the Lord,"[97] there is no Scriptural record of any offerings to the Lord for the period of almost two thousand years between the birth of Seth and Noah's offerings after he disembarked from the ark after the flood. That is not to say offerings were not made, but there is no Scriptural record of any offerings. This reality may be a contributing factor to the increase of wickedness on the earth.

A second factor is the appearance of giants among the families of the earth. The Scripture says, "There were giants on the earth in those days, and also afterward, when the sons of God came into the daughters of men, and they bore *children* to them. Those *were* the mighty men who *were* of old, men of renown."[98] The "sons of God" have been much debated and some scholars consider them to be members of the class of angelic beings that came before God in the days of Job.

---

94. Matt. 6:24.
95. Gen. 6:5-6.
96. Heb. 11:5.
97. Gen. 4:25-26.
98. Gen. 6:4.

"Now there was a day when the sons of God came to present them-selves before the LORD, and Satan also came among them."[99] In other words "sons of God" in the Genesis six passage may refer to angelic beings who had served in the heavenly council of God. It seems pos-sible that a time came when some of those angelic beings fell from their former estate and co-habited with the beautiful daughters of men, and their offspring were giants.[100] Even though this is contro-versial, the Scripture does speak of "giants" and "sons of God" in the same verse. Some scholars say that the fallen angelic beings also con-tributed to the corruption and wickedness of men through teaching occultic practices, linking Genesis 6:1-4 together with 2 Peter 2:1-5.[101] One thing is for sure, the wickedness of man was so great that God determined to destroy both man and beast, creeping things and birds of the air, except for Noah and his wife with their three sons and their wives and the animals on the ark, because "Noah found grace in the eyes of the Lord."[102]

Noah with his family and the animals were on the ark for a total of three hundred and seventy-one days.[103] After the flood Noah built an altar and offered sacrifices. "And the LORD smelled a soothing aroma. Then the LORD said in His heart, "I will never again curse the ground for man's sake, although the imagination of man's heart

---

99. Job 1:6, 2:1.

100. 2 Peter 2:4; Jude 8.

101. Michael S. Heiser, *The Unseen Realm: Recovering the Supernatural Worldview of the Bible* (Bellingham, WA: Lexham Press, 2015), 108-109.

102. Gen. 6:7-12.

103. John C. Whitcomb, Jr. and Henry M. Morris, *The Genesis Flood: The Biblical Record and Its Scientific Implications* (Philadelphia, PA: The Presbyterian and Reformed Publishing Co., 1974), 3.

is evil from his youth; nor will I again destroy every living thing as I have done."[104] Then the Lord spoke to Noah saying,

> (9) "'And as for Me, behold, I establish My covenant with you and with your descendants after you, (10) and with every living creature that *is* with you: the birds, the cattle, and every beast of the earth with you, of all that go out of the ark, every beast of the earth. (11) Thus, I establish My covenant with you: Never again shall all flesh be cut off by the waters of the flood; never again shall there be a flood to destroy the earth." (12) And God said: "This *is* the sign of the covenant which I make between Me and you, and every living creature that *is* with you, for perpetual generations: (13) I set My rainbow in the cloud, and it shall be for the sign of the covenant between Me and the earth. (14) It shall be, when I bring a cloud over the earth, that the rainbow shall be seen in the cloud; (15) and I will remember My covenant which *is* between Me and you and every living creature of all flesh; the waters shall never again become a flood to destroy all flesh. (16) The rainbow shall be in the cloud, and I will look on it to remember the everlasting covenant between God and every living creature of all flesh that *is* on the earth.' (17) And God said to Noah, 'This *is* the sign of the covenant which I have established between Me and all flesh that *is* on the earth.'" (Genesis 9:7-17)

104. Gen. 8:21.

The flood and the covenant God made with Noah are major turning points in the history of God's relationship with mankind. Now there would be a new beginning with Noah and his family repopulating the earth. Whereas previously God had judged mankind in one massive flood. But from now on God would relate to man on a more individual basis. The rainbow would be the sign of God's covenantal relationship with all people.[105] As Noah's sons and their families multiplied, challenges to God's sovereignty arose. God's response to those challenges will be discussed in the following chapters. But for now, we will summarize the main points of this chapter.

Summary:

First, God created mankind in His own image and likeness. It is clear from the record of creation in Genesis chapters one and two that all things created including Adam were good, even very good.[106] Adam was created from the ground and God breathed His life into Adam's body and he became a living soul. Eve was not created from the ground, but God formed her from a rib taken from Adam's body. Mankind did not evolve from some lower form of being over thousands or millions of years. Neither is man simply an animal with some higher capacities than other animals. Man is a son of God,[107] created in the image and likeness of God with the capacity to serve as His stewards over the earth and worship God in the beauty of holiness.

Second, God did not create sin nor death. God did plant the tree of life and the tree of the knowledge of good and evil in the midst of

---

105. Gen. 9:5-9.
106. Gen. 1:31.
107. Luke 3:38.

the garden. "And the LORD God commanded the man, saying, 'Of every tree of the garden you may freely eat; but of the tree of the knowledge of good and evil you shall not eat, for in the day that you eat of it you shall surely die.'"[108]

Third, a very subtle creature called the "serpent" entered the Garden of Eden and tempted Eve to eat the forbidden fruit. The identification of the serpent is further clarified as "... the dragon, that serpent of old, who is *the* Devil and Satan...."[109] Satan continues to spearhead the enmity and conflict between the seed of the serpent and the seed of the woman. It is my conviction that this evil being was in opposition to God prior to the seven days of creation as recorded in Genesis one and two and will eventually end in the "lake of fire and brimstone."[110] At the cross the seed of the serpent bruised the heel of the seed of the woman and the seed of the woman bruised the head of the serpent, and that evil being is destined for everlasting torment.[111]

Fourth, Adam did eat of the fruit from the tree of the knowledge of good and evil. Eating that which God had forbidden was an act of disobedience, a moral violation of God's holy nature which is sin. The wages of sin is death. The definition of death is separation from God the one and only source of life. Adam's disobedience is the origin of sin and death in the earth. Adam and Eve were also driven from the Garden of Eden and separated from the manifest presence of God. However, because of God's plan for the triumph of the seed of the woman over sin and death, Adam and all mankind have hope.[112] And hope is the substance of faith and faith is what pleases God. Because

---

108. Gen. 2:16-17.
109. Rev. 20:2
110. Rev. 20:10.
111. Matt. 8:29.
112. Rom. 8:20.

you have hope, no matter how frustrating and grievous things may seem to you today, hope in God because the best is yet to come!

Fifth, God was prepared to atone for Adam's sin through the shedding of the blood of a substitutionary sacrifice that would die in Adam's place. The blood shed resulting in the death of an animal made an atonement for Adam's sin, and the skin of the animal provided a covering for his naked body. The shedding of the blood of a substitutionary sacrifice was according to the terms of the everlasting covenant between the members of the Godhead before time began.[113] When God provided an atonement for Adam, He was prophetically looking forward to the day when on the cross, Jesus the Lamb of God, who knew no sin would be made sin for us, that we might be made the righteousness of God in Him.[114]

Sixth, Adam and Eve's sin changed their physical nature from innocence and purity to sinner and corruption. Their spirits died that day because their sin of disobedience separated them from God the source of life. Therefore, their spirit would no longer have the capacity to guide their attitudes and actions. Now, sin infected their flesh which would war in defiance against the Spirit of God. And what they willed to do they would not do, and that which they willed not to do, that they would do.[115] Therefore, Adam and all others are to look through the eyes of faith to the cross upon which Jesus, the seed of the woman died to deliver us from this body of death.[116]

Seventh, Adam and Eve would pass their sin nature on to their children. Therefore, the children do not sin and become sinners. They are born with a sin nature and because they have a sin nature,

113. Heb. 13:20.
114. John 1:29; 2 Cor. 5:21.
115. Rom. 7:19-24.
116. Rom. 7:24-25.

they commit sin. Cain, their first son, killed his brother Abel. As the generations passed sin increased on the earth "until every intent of the thoughts of man's heart was only evil continually."[117] Therefore, God sent a flood to destroy all men, animals, and birds. "But Noah found grace in the eyes of the Lord"[118] and was preserved alive on the ark with his wife, three sons and their wives, as well as a limited number of all kinds of animals and birds.

The Spirit of the Lord hid all seven of these factors in the mystery of the cross. But "the natural man does not receive the things of the Spirit of God, for they are foolishness to him; nor can he know *them*, because they are spiritually discerned."[119] "But God has revealed *them* to us through His Spirit. For the Spirit searches all things, yes, the deep things of God."[120] "These things we also speak, not in words which man's wisdom teaches, but which the Holy Spirit teaches, comparing spiritual things with spiritual."[121]

After Noah disembarked from the ark, he built an altar and offered sacrifices unto the Lord. "And the LORD smelled a soothing aroma. Then the LORD said in His heart, 'I will never again curse the ground for man's sake, although the imagination of man's heart *is* evil from his youth; nor will I again destroy every living thing as I have done.'"[122] Then the Lord made a covenant with Noah and his descendants. "And God said: 'This *is* the sign of the covenant which I make between Me and you, and every living creature that *is* with you,

---

117. Gen. 6:5
118. Gen. 6:18.
119. 1 Cor. 2:14.
120. 1 Cor. 2:10.
121. 1 Cor. 2:13.
122. Gen. 8:21.

for perpetual generations: I set My rainbow in the cloud, and it shall be for the sign of the covenant between Me and the earth.'"[123]

How great to know that our God so loves us that He has set Himself in a covenant to never again destroy humanity with a world-wide flood, but has made every provision for our salvation, even in the face of a relentless adversary. However, God's redemptive provisions can only be grasp through faith. In the next chapter we will discuss how God overcame challenges to His sovereignty and continued unveiling His plan of redemption through shadows of the cross, as written in the Old Testament.

---

123. Gen. 9:12-13.

The Foreshadows
of the Cross

"Therefore, when He came into the world, He said:
'Sacrifice and offering You did not desire, but a body You
have prepared for Me. In burnt offerings and sacrifices for
sin You had no pleasure.' Then I said, 'Behold, I have come-
- In the volume of the book it is written of Me-- To do Your
will, O God.'" (Hebrews 10:5-7)

"For I delivered to you first of all that which I also
received: that Christ died for our sins according to
the Scriptures, and that He was buried, and that He
rose again the third day according to the Scriptures,"
(1 Corinthians 15:3-4)

GOD IS ETERNAL AND a Father by nature. His desire is to have a
family of sons and daughters that love Him with all their heart and
soul. The reality is that you were in the heart of God before He said,
"Let there be light."[124] In eternity past the members of the Godhead
established the everlasting covenant in which they purposed the creation and redemption of a royal family in the image and likeness of

---

124. Gen. 1:3.

God. The everlasting covenant included the necessity of the cross upon which our Savior would die. The cross was not an afterthought or some secondary action to remedy the sin problem that occurred when Adam ate the forbidden fruit. The Scriptures reveal that Jesus was "the Lamb slain from the foundation of the world."[125] And Jesus' death on the cross is foreshadowed in the Old Testament through many of God's redemptive relationships. R. C. Lenski states, "But 'according to the Scriptures' includes everything that was foretold concerning the significance and the efficacy of Christ's death; when Christ died, all of this, too, became everlasting reality."[126] Therefore, even the Old Testament sacrifices foreshadow or prefigure the ultimate sacrifice of God's only begotten Son. Kevin J. Conner and Ken Malmin state,

> God, knowing the end from the beginning, was able to cause the writing of the Old Testament to be done in such a way that many of its elements were meant to be viewed as anticipative of that which was to come in the New Testament.... In the writing of scripture God caused the recording of history to be such that certain persons are meant to be viewed as prefiguring another person to come. These persons can be seen as foreshadows in either their character, office, function or relationship to the history of redemption.[127]

---

125. Rev. 13:8.

126. R. C. H. Lenski, *The Interpretation of St. Paul's First and Second Epistle to the Corinthians* (Minneapolis, MN: Augsburg Publishing House, 1963), 631.

127. Kevin J. Conner and Ken Malmin, *Interpreting the Scriptures: A Textbook on How to Interpret the Bible* (Portland, OR: BT Publishing, 1983), 136.

This chapter will focus on stories from the Old Testament Scriptures that foreshadow the cross of Christ. For example, Ada R. Habershon states, "The ark passing through the waters of the flood was a type of death, the resting of the ark on Mt. Ararat, and Noah stepping forth on to the new earth would prefigure resurrection life."[128] These prophetic pictures include Jacob's favorite son Joseph, being hated by his brothers and thrown in a pit. Then he was raised out of the pit and sold for twenty shekels of silver. But it was all in the redemptive plan of God for Joseph to prepare for the survival of the family, just as Jesus was placed in the grave and then raised out of that grave and has gone ahead of us into heaven to prepare a place for us.[129] Joseph later told his brothers; "Do not be afraid, for *am* I in the place of God? But as for you, you meant evil against me; *but* God meant it for good, in order to bring it about as *it is* this day, to save many people alive."[130] The cross was foreshadowed by Aaron's rod that was simply a dead stick of wood that was placed by Moses before the Lord in the Tabernacle along with one rod from each of the heads of the other eleven tribes of Israel. "The next day that Moses went into the tabernacle of witness, and behold, the rod of Aaron, of the house of Levi, had sprouted and put forth buds, had produced blossoms and yielded ripe almonds."[131] Resurrection life brings fruitful authority whereby we reign through Jesus Christ.[132] The three Hebrew children being thrown into the fiery furnace and walked out of that furnace without even the smell of fire, picture resurrection

---

128. Ada R. Habershon, *The Study of the Types* (Grand Rapids, MI: Kregel Publications, 1974), 46.

129. John 14:3-4.

130. Gen. 50:19-20.

131. Num. 17:8.

132. Rom. 5:17.

life that foreshadows some aspects of the crucifixion and resurrection of Jesus.[133]

Many other Old Testament narratives foreshadow the cross of Christ. One of the most beautiful examples is that of Abraham offering his promised son Isaac on an altar to the Lord. To gain a richer understanding of this story we will begin with Genesis chapters ten and eleven, the narrative following the covenant that God made with Noah after the flood.

From Noah to Abraham:

"Noah lived after the flood three hundred and fifty years."[134] From the time Noah disembarked from the ark until the call of Abraham was a period of about 400 years. The main events of those years are squeezed into the narrative of Genesis chapters 10 and 11. The events of these two chapters overlap each other. To gain a more complete understanding of what transpired during those years requires that we place the personalities and events of those two chapters together as best as we can in a sequential narrative. John Walton states, "In chapter 11, the narrator moves backward in time to tell the story of how these nations initially became separate from a unified people who developed subsequent to the time of Noah."[135] The Scriptures reveal some significant issues in this narrative that we need to search out. Proverbs states, "*It is* the glory of God to conceal a matter, but the glory of kings *is* to search out a matter."[136]

---

133. Dan. 3:27.
134. Gen. 9:28.
135. Walton, *Genesis: The NIV Application Commentary*, 2001, 376.
136. Prov. 25:2.

We will consider four major factors in these two chapters that will contribute to a better understanding of the significance of the story of Abraham and Isaac. First, Nimrod is given special mention. Nimrod is the son of Cush, and the grandson of Ham. Henry M. Morris gives this insight:

> Cush, as Ham's oldest son, had apparently resented this curse (*The curse that Noah placed upon Ham's son Canaan*)[137] more and more as the years pass by. By the time Nimrod was born, the resentment had become so strong that he gave his son a name meaning "Let us rebel!" The inference is that Cush trained Nimrod from childhood to be a leader in a planned and organized rebellion against God's purposes for mankind."[138] (Emphasis mine).

Nimrod is singled out as "a mighty hunter before the LORD; therefore, it is said, 'Like Nimrod the mighty hunter before the LORD.' And the beginning of his kingdom was Babel, Erech, Accad, and Calneh, in the land of Shinar."[139] The land of Shinar is considered to be where the tower of Babel was erected, and "Babel is the Hebrew name for Babylon."[140] Babylon is later referred to in Scripture as "THE MOTHER OF HARLOTS AND OF THE ABOMINATIONS OF THE EARTH."[141] In other words after the flood in the days of Noah there arose an organized rebellion against God. That rebellion resulted in

137. Gen. 9:24-25.

138. Morris, *The Genesis Record*, 251.

139. Gen. 10:9-10

140. David R. Shepherd, Editor-in-Chief, *Shepherd's Notes: Genesis* (Nashville, TN: Broadman & Holman Publishers, 197), 37.

141. Rev. 17:5.

men building the Tower of Babel. Nimrod seems to have had a leadership role in that rebellion because the beginning of his kingdom was Babel in the Land of Shinar. His kingdom of Babel perpetuated a negative impact on the inhabitants of that region, influencing the lives of men and women all over the world against the purposes of God. Michael S. Heisler states,

> Nimrod is cast as the progenitor of the civilizations of Assyria and Babylon (Gen. 10:6-12) .... Assyria and Babylon are the two civilizations that will later destroy the dream of the earthly kingdom of God in Israel, dismantling, respectively, the northern kingdom (Israel) and southern kingdom (Judah).[142]

Second, the tower of Babel was built in the land of Shinar.[143] It is possible that Nimrod was an antichrist personality that contributed leadership in the building of the tower of Babel. Men in their arrogance sought to make a name for themselves in organized rebellion against God. John Walton states, "We can affirm that it occurred prior to the development of many of the nations referred to in chapter 10."[144]

It was at Babel that God moved in judgement by confusing the people's language and scattered them over the face of the earth.[145] This point demonstrates that in the repopulation of the earth after the flood, men in their self-centered pride organized in a concerted rebellion, refusing to accept God's rule over them. If left unchecked,

---

142. Heiser, *The Unseen Realm*, 111.
143. Gen. 11:1-9.
144. Walton, *Genesis: The NIV Application Commentary*, 371.
145. Gen. 11:1-9.

the wickedness at Babel would have corrupted all people again and God's plan to have a royal family in His image would have been destroyed. Therefore, God confused their language, so they did not understand one another's speech and scattered them abroad over the face of the earth.[146] Thus, nations were formed for the first time in the history of the world.[147]

Third, the first mention of "nations" in the Scriptures is found in Genesis 10:5. The word "nations" in this context implies the establishment of some form of civil government in a specific geographic location with a specific tribe or ethnic group. Before the flood there is no record of nations. But wickedness progressed unrestrained until the flood in Noah's time. Following the flood all people of the world descended from Noah's sons, Shem, Ham, and Japheth. And from their descendants "the nations were divided on the earth after the flood."[148] It was at the Tower of Babel that God confused the languages and scattered families into nations.[149] It was not God's highest desire to establish civil governments. However, civil governments were a temporary accommodation until God could raise up a people who loved Him enough to obey and serve Him and each other without having to be policed.[150] When God established the nation of Israel at Mt. Sinai, it was a covenantal relationship between Himself and the Children of Israel. There were priest, elders, judges, and prophets like Moses, but no king nor policemen. Civil governments, including kings and policeman are ministers authorized by God to keep order and restrain anarchy among the citizens of the nations until God's

146. Gen. 11:6-9.
147. Gen. 10:5.
148. Gen 10:32.
149. Gen. 11:6-8.
150. Mark 12:28-31.

redemptive purposes are complete.[151] Once His redemptive purposes are complete there will be no further need for police officers. When Jesus returns all people on the earth will bow their knees to Him, the Prince of Peace. He will rule and reign with His bride, the Church, for a thousand years as a theocracy, not as a civil government like the governments we are familiar with today.

Fourth, the nations of the world from the time of Genesis 10 and 11 until the second coming of Jesus will be governed through an indirect relationship with God. Following the judgment at the tower of Babel, our sovereign Lord administers His government over the nations of the world through principalities and powers. The Scripture states, "When the Most High gave to the nations their inheritance, when he divided mankind, he fixed the borders of the peoples according to the number of the sons of God. But the Lord's portion is his people, Jacob his allotted heritage." (Deut. 32:8-9 English Standard Version). M. Heisler states,

> Deuteronomy 32:8–9 describes how Yahweh's dispersal of the nations at Babel resulted in his *disinheriting* those nations as his people. This is the Old Testament equivalent of Romans 1:18–25, a familiar passage wherein God "gave [humankind] over" to their persistent rebellion. The statement in Deuteronomy 32:9 that "the Lord's [i.e., Yahweh's] portion is his people, Jacob his allotted heritage" tips us off that a contrast in affection and ownership is intended. Yahweh in effect decided that the people of the world's nations were no longer going to be in

---

151. Rom. 13:1-10.

relationship to him. He would begin anew. He would enter covenant relationship with a new people that did not yet exist: Israel.[152]

Abraham and Isaac:

Having considered these four factors; the rise of Nimrod, the rebellion at the tower of Babel, the establishment of nations, and the divine governing of the nations of the world through principalities and powers sets the stage upon which Abram was called by God. God reached into the midst of the rebellious nations choosing and calling one man, Abram, out of his homeland and planting him like a seed in the foreign soil of Canaan.

> Now the LORD had said to Abram: 'Get out of your country, from your family and from your father's house, to a land that I will show you. I will make you a great nation; I will bless you and make your name great; And you shall be a blessing. I will bless those who bless you, And I will curse him who curses you; And in you all the families of the earth shall be blessed.' (Genesis 12:1-3).

"By faith Abraham obeyed when he was called to go out to the place which he would receive as an inheritance. And he went out, not knowing where he was going."[153] He was seventy-five years old when he reached the land of Canaan. Abram and his wife Sarah had no children. But God promised Abram that He would make him become

---

152. Heiser, *The Unseen Realm*, 113.
153. Heb. 11:8.

a great nation. To affirm that promise God entered into an unconditional covenant with Abram. In that covenant God changed Abram's name to Abraham which means "father of many nations."[154] God said, "I will make you exceedingly fruitful; and I will make nations of you, and kings shall come from you."[155] Then God gave Abraham circumcision as the sign of His covenant and the promise of a son to be born to him and Sarah.[156] "Abraham believed in the LORD, and He accounted it to him for righteousness."[157]

"Abraham did not waver at the promise of God through unbelief, but was strengthened in faith, giving glory to God, and being fully convinced that what He had promised He was also able to perform."[158] The point is that in the midst of a world that was characterized by self-centered rebellion against God, Abraham believed and trusted God. Although he and Sarah were beyond child-bearing age he was strengthened in faith, believing that what God promised He would do. Finally, Abraham "was one hundred years old when his son Isaac was born to him. And Sarah said, 'God has made me laugh, *and* all who hear will laugh with me.' ... 'I have borne *him* a son in his old age.'"[159]

We gain three significant insights from this story. **First**, out of all the people in the world God by His grace chose to call Abraham out of the midst of the unbelieving world, setting him apart for His redemptive purposes. **Second,** the nations of the world were hostile against God, but He continued fulfilling His purpose of having a

---

154. Gen. 17:5, 15:1-21.
155. Gen. 17:6-7.
156. Gen. 17:1-22.
157. Gen. 15:6; Rom. 4:3.
158. Rom. 4:20-21.
159. Gem. 21:5-7.

family of sons and daughters separate from the surrounding nations through the unconditional covenant with Abraham, promising him a son. **Third**, Abraham's enduring faith was rewarded with the supernatural conception **and birth of a son,** Isaac, even though "Abraham and Sarah were old, well advanced in age; *and* Sarah had passed the age of childbearing."[160] The birth of Isaac brought Abraham and Sarah great joy. Abraham's call, covenant, and the conception and birth of his son, Isaac, foreshadow the supernatural intervention of God in bringing His own Son, our Savior, Jesus, into the world.

It was in the city of Nazareth, before Joseph and Mary were married, that God sent the angel Gabriel to a distant granddaughter of Abraham, named Mary. **First**, Gabriel announced to Mary that among all the women in the world, God had chosen her. He proclaimed, "Rejoice, highly favored *one*, the Lord *is* with you; blessed *are* you among women!"[161] **Second**, Mary, being a granddaughter of Abraham, was already in a covenant with God. Gabriel continued, "And behold, you will conceive in your womb and bring forth a Son and shall call His name JESUS."[162] Since Mary was not married it would take a supernatural intervention of God for her to have a son. Therefore, she asked, "How can this be, since I do not know a man?"[163] **Third**, Gabriel answered Mary saying, "*The* Holy Spirit will come upon you, and the power of the Highest will overshadow you; therefore, also, that Holy One who is to be born will be called the Son of God."[164] Mary then expressed faith in God by saying, "'Let it be unto

---

160. Gen. 18:11.
161. Luke 1:28.
162. Luke 1:31.
163. Luke 1:34.
164. Luke 1:35.

me according to your word.' And the angel departed from her."[165] Rather than facing the world with disgrace or shame, she proclaimed her joyful faith to her cousin Elizabeth saying, "My soul magnifies the Lord, and my spirit has rejoiced in God my Savior."[166]

During the time when Abraham was living in Beersheba, he called on the name of the Lord "the Everlasting God."[167] In other words, Abraham was enjoying his son, Isaac, and the blessing of prosperity and security his covenant with God. However, things were about to change, because "it came to pass after these things that God tested Abraham."[168] As the birth of Isaac foreshadowed the birth of Jesus, so also did God's command for Abraham to now offer up his son Isaac on the mountains of Moriah. M. R. De Haan makes these comments, "All Abraham's love centered on Isaac.... Jesus, too, was well-beloved of the Father."[169] At the baptism of Jesus God said, "You are My beloved Son; in You I am well pleased."[170] But now Abraham's test; God said, "Take now your son, your only *son* Isaac, whom you love, and go to the land of Moriah, and offer him there as a burnt offering on one of the mountains of which I shall tell you."[171] The mountains of Moriah seen to include the city of Jerusalem where Jesus was crucified. In fact, "Solomon began to build the house of the LORD at Jerusalem on Mount Moriah, where *the Lord* had appeared to his father David,

---

165. Luke 1:38.

166. Luke 1:46-47.

167. Gen. 21:23.

168. Gen. 22:1.

169. M. R. De Haan, *Portraits of Christ in Genesis* (Grand Rapids, MI: Kregel Publications, 1995), 135.

170. Luke 3:22.

171. Gen. 22:2.

at the place that David had prepared on the threshing floor of Ornan the Jebusite."[172]

Abraham received the command from God to offer up his son Isaac; you can imagine the stress of the test as obedient Abraham travels for three days to the place where God would show him. The Bible never reveals what he said to Sarah about offering their son before he left home. You can only imagine what may have been going through his mind during that three-day journey with his son and servants. It was probably an emotionally demanding journey as he kept looking at Isaac through the eyes of faith and seeing him as the sacrifice. This is the son "whom Abraham loved."[173] This is the first mention of "love" in the Scripture. The love of a father for his "only begotten son."[174] Would Abraham really offer his son or save him? Do you wonder about the intensity of Abraham's thoughts and the trial of his faith as they journeyed? Remember, it was such an intense time when Jesus was on the cross that "from the sixth hour until the ninth hour there was darkness over all the land."[175] There were hours of agony from the Garden of Gethsemane until on the cross Jesus finally said, "It is finished."[176] What do you think was on the heart of God the Father as He sacrificed His only begotten Son for our sin? Then God the Father had to experience the three days His Son's sacrificial body remained lifeless in the grave. In writing about Abraham and Isaac foreshadowing God the Father offering His only begotten Jesus on the cross, A. W. Pink states,

---

172. 2 Chro. 3:1.
173. Gen. 22:2.
174. Heb. 11:17; John 3:16.
175. Matt. 27:45.
.176. John 19:30.

Here it was that God first revealed the necessity for a human victim to expiate sin, for as it was man that had sinned, it must be by man, and not by sacrifice of beast, that divine justice would be satisfied.... This is one of the very few Old Testament types that brings before us not only God the Son but also God the Father. Here, as nowhere else, we are shown the Father's heart. Here it is that we get such a wonderful foreshadowing of the divine side of Calvary.[177]

Abraham arriving near the place God had directed, took Isaac, the wood, and the fire, and proceeded to the spot where Abraham built an altar. He bound Isaac and laid him on the altar. At this point Isaac himself is a type of Christ and we could say, "He was led as a lamb to the slaughter, and as a sheep before its shearers is silent, so he opened not His mouth."[178] Then Abraham raised his hand with the knife to slay his son. Suddenly, the Angel of the Lord called to him and said, "Do not lay your hand on the lad, or do anything to him; for now I know that you fear God, since you have not withheld your son, your only *son*, from Me."[179] These words from the Angel of the Lord are full proof of Abraham's faith and obedience. The Angel of the Lord could have added, "Even as the heavenly Father will not withhold His only and well-beloved Son as the great provision for man's redemption." How beautifully this also foreshadows the crucifixion of Jesus.

Abraham lifted up his eyes and there in the thicket was a ram caught in thorns wrapped around its head. God had provided a substitute for Isaac. Abraham then offered the ram in the place of

177. Pink, *Gleanings in Genesis*, 221-222.
178. Isa. 53:7.
179. Gen. 22:12.

Isaac. "And Abraham called the name of the place, The-LORD-Will-Provide; as it is said *to* this day, "In the Mount of The LORD it shall be provided."[180] Ken Hemphill states,

> This is the name Jehovah-Jireh. The Hebrew word *jireh* can be translated "to see." You wonder what the connection is between "seeing" and "providing." Actually, we can make the connection even in the English noun *provision*. It is a compound of two Latin words which taken together mean "to see beforehand." Thus "pro-vision" would mean "to see before." In God's case, He had anticipated, or seen beforehand Abraham's need for a sacrifice and thus had personally provided one. Before the foundation of the world, God had prior vision of man's later sin and rebellion. Seeing man's need, He made provision for our redemption by providing a Lamb of sacrifice, His only Son.[181]

"By faith Abraham, when he was tested, offered up Isaac… concluding that God *was* able to raise *him* up, even from the dead, from which he also received him in a figurative sense."[182] A. W. Pink states,

> From this scripture we learn that Genesis 22 presents to us in type not only Christ offered upon the altar, but Christ raised again from the dead, and that

---

180. Gen. 22:14.

181. Ken Hemphill, *The Names of God* (Nashville, TN: Broadman & Holman Publishers, 2001), 85-86.

182. Heb. 11:17-19.

on the third day, too, for it was on "the third day" Abraham received Isaac back again, for during the three days that had elapsed from the time Abraham received the command from God to offer him up as a burnt offering, his son was as good as dead to him.[183]

In the New Testament Abraham is declared to be the father of those who live by faith.[184] Abraham's faith and obedience through offering up his son Isaac is a foreshadow of God's redemptive plan to offer up His only begotten Son. This is just one Old Testament example of our heavenly Father giving all mankind hope by foreshadowing the crucifixion and resurrection of His Son, that would take place in about two-thousand years. New Testament believers are not dependent upon shadows for our redemption, but our faith is anchored in the reality of our crucified and risen Savior Jesus Christ. He is our true substitute that died on the cross in our place. He is risen from the dead for our justification. Because He lives, we shall live also![185]

Therefore, as believers journeying through this present world and personally experiencing the fulfillment of God's redemptive plans and promises, we enter with Abraham into the fellowship of overcoming faith. Participating in the redemptive power of the cross we can exclaim: "Then our mouth was filled with laughter, and our tongue with singing. Then they said among the nations, 'The LORD has done great things for them.'"[186] When speaking of trust in the crucified and resurrected Lord Jesus Christ, Leon Morris states,

183. Pink, *Gleanings in Genesis,* 225.
184. Rom. 4:16.
185. John 14:19.
186. Psa. 126:2.

"It transforms men from being slaves to sin to being the people of God."[187]

The Passover Lamb:

Another beautiful example that foreshadows the cross in the redemptive ministry of Jesus is "the Passover lamb" sacrificed by the Children of Israel on that fateful night in Egypt.[188] Abraham's family, led by his grandson Jacob, moved to Egypt because of a severe famine in Canaan. There, in Egypt, Jacob's son Joseph, by God's marvelous providence had risen to a position of political power. Joseph provided for his father and brothers, and Jacob's family prospered. But the time came when a Pharaoh reigned over Egypt who did not know Joseph and that Pharaoh enslaved the Children of Israel. However, in the process of time God raised up Moses as His spokesman to deliver the Children of Israel from their Egyptian bondage.

God sent Moses with clear instructions; "Say to the children of Israel: 'I *am* the LORD; I will bring you out from under the burdens of the Egyptians, I will rescue you from their bondage, and I will redeem you with an outstretched arm and with great judgments.'"[189] Keep in mind that sin is not the issue being resolved in the Passover narrative. The primary issue is God redeeming and delivering the nation of Israel from Egyptian bondage was so they could freely worship Him as His own covenant nation. In other words, God was purchasing the children of Israel at the price of the blood of the Passover lamb for Himself from among the nations of the world. Although sin

---

187. Leon Morris, *The Apostolic Preaching of the Cross* (Grand Rapids, MI: William B. Eerdmans Publishing Co., 1965), 131.

188. Exod. 12:16-27.

189. Exod. 6:6.

was not specifically being dealt at the Passover, it would be fully dealt with at Mt. Sinai. The redemptive story of the Passover is recorded in Exodus, chapters 11 through 14.

Upon Moses' arrival in Egypt and his request before Pharaoh to release the Children of Israel, their bondage became even more severe. Therefore, Moses imposed God ordained plagues upon the Egyptians and after nine plagues Pharaoh still refused to release the Children of Israel. Moses then proceeded with the tenth and final plague, the Passover, and the death of the firstborn in each household not protected by the blood of the Passover lamb.[190] The Passover finalized the release of the Children of Israel from their Egyptian bondage so they could go and hold a feast to the God of Abraham, Isaac, and Jacob.[191]

When the Lord instituted the Passover, He said, "This month shall be your beginning of months; it shall be the first month of the year to you."[192] In other words, the Lord determined Passover as the birthday of Israel as a nation.[193] Up until this time Abraham and his family were in a covenantal relationship with the Lord which set them apart from the other families of the world. Jacob's family consisted of seventy souls when they moved to Egypt.[194] They lived in the Egyptian region of Goshen which served as a womb for the development of a seventy-member family into twelve tribes with a population of over a million. Therefore, God through the institution of the Passover was taking a redemptive step in the transformation of Abraham's family of twelve tribes into "a kingdom of priest and a holy nation."[195] It was

---

190. Exod. 11:1-5.
191. Exod. 5:1, 10:9.
192. Exod. 12:2.
193. Hosea 11:1; Isa. 43:15.
194. Gen. 46:27.
195. Exod. 19:6.

with the blood of the Passover lamb the Lord purchased Israel saying, "all the firstborn, whatever opens the womb among the children of Israel, both man and beast; it is Mine." The firstborn represents the strength of a nation.

It was from this first Passover that Israel's existence as a nation was to be counted and celebrated as a memorial throughout their generations.[196] After their arrival at Mount Sinai God formalized His relationship with the Children of Israel as a nation through the Mosaic covenant. The terms of the Mosaic covenant included the Law, the privileges and responsibilities of the priesthood, offerings, feasts, and the authorization to build the tabernacle according to the heavenly pattern so God could dwell in their midst. This would be the first time since the Garden of Eden that God dwelt on earth among men.

God was redeeming the children of Israel from their Egyptian bondage and gathering them unto Himself as a holy nation to worship Him. His intention was for them to serve as His witness amidst a world of nations that were hostile to Him. E. F. Harrison provides these insights.

> God's deliverance of his people from Egypt is spoken of as a redemption (Exod. 6:6; 15:13), and he is Israel's Redeemer (Ps. 78:35). The emphasis here may well be upon the great output of strength needed to accomplish this objective—strength which itself serves as a kind of ransom price.... The ransom idea may well be the assumed factor that is kept in the background by the very prominence given to the element of power

196. Exod. 12:14.

needed for deliverance.... No word in the Christian vocabulary deserves to be held more precious than Redeemer, for even more than Savior it reminds the child of God that his salvation has been purchased at a great and personal cost....[197]

A key factor to consider at this juncture is Israel's deliverance from bondage. Sin in terms of forgiveness or justification is not the issue being dealt with at the Feast of Passover. The word "sin" is not once mentioned at all in the discussion of the Passover (Exodus 11-14). The Children of Israel were already in a covenantal relationship with God through the Abrahamic covenant. The sign of their covenant was circumcision. And no uncircumcised person was permitted to eat of the Passover Lamb.[198] The issue at stake here is "bondage." The Egyptian bondage forced them to work under the control of taskmasters, which was demanding and painfully stressful. But the greater issue was they were not free to worship God. Therefore, God redeemed the Children of Israel from their Egyptian bondage so they could freely worship Him.[199] Just as God first sets us free from sin and then delivers us "from the power of darkness and conveys us into the kingdom of the Son of His love."[200] The life of the Passover lamb was the redemptive price or the full market price that God paid to purchase Israel from Egyptian bondage, liberating them to freely worship Him.

---

197. F. F. Harrison, *Redeemer, Redemption* in "Evangelical Dictionary of Theology: Second Edition", by Walter A. Elwell (Grand Rapids, MI: Baker Academic, 2001), 994.
198. Exod. 12:48.
199. Exod. 5:1-4, 10:9.
200. Col. 1:13.

The Lord had a high purpose for the Children of Israel and that was for them to worship and serve Him as a holy nation. God considered Israel His son, His firstborn.[201] God intended for His family to dwell among the nations of the world, bearing testimony to His greatness. God promised Abraham that in him "all the families of the earth shall be blessed." God intended for His Children to be an example and a light to all the other nations, and thus attract them to seek a relationship with God. He wanted the Children of Israel to reveal the blessings of living in a covenantal relationship with His Lordship.

Sinful mankind is morally bankrupt and cannot deliver himself from the bondage of sin and darkness. Sin not only separated man from God, which is spiritual death. But when man sinned, he forfeited his God given dominion over the earth to the devil, and the devil became "the ruler of this world."[202] The New Testament states, "The whole world lies under the sway of the wicked one."[203] Therefore, mankind needs someone who is willing and able to redeem him from the bondage of this evil taskmaster. God in His loving mercy chose to redeem mankind by paying the ransom price to Himself and giving His only begotten Son to die as our substitute on the cross. Jesus is our Deliverer, our Passover.[204] To be free from our taskmaster we must receive the circumcision of our hearts, because a relationship with God is first and foremost a heart issue.[205] That circumcision is made possible through faith in the crucified and risen Savior. The Holy Spirit administers the circumcision to your heart when you, by faith's confession, receive Jesus Christ as your personal Savior.

201. Exod. 4:22-23.
202. John 12:31.
203. 1 John 5:19.
204. 1 Cor. 5:7.
205. Matt. 22:37-40.

> In Him you were also circumcised with the circum-
> cision made without hands, by putting off the body
> of the sins of the flesh, by the circumcision of Christ,
> buried with Him in baptism, in which you also were
> raised with *Him* through faith in the working of God,
> who raised Him from the dead. And you, being dead
> in your trespasses and the uncircumcision of your
> flesh, He has made alive together with Him, hav-
> ing forgiven you all trespasses, having wiped out the
> handwriting of requirements that was against us,
> which was contrary to us. And He has taken it out
> of the way, having nailed it to the cross. (Colossians
> 2:11-14)

Jesus Christ our Passover, has liberated each believer from the dominion of sin and from the bondage of the prince of power of the air.[206] God our Father, through the ministry of Jesus our Savior delivers "us from the power of darkness and conveys us into the kingdom of the Son of His love."[207] "Therefore, if the Son makes you free, you shall be free indeed."[208] However, freedom from the bondage of our taskmaster requires that each believer in Jesus Christ take responsibility for the choices that he or she makes. The devil is a "tempter", and each believer must resist the devil and draw near to God.[209] "Stand fast therefore in the liberty by which Christ has made us free, and do not be entangled again with a yoke of bondage."[210] The Holy

---

206. Eph. 2:1-7.
207. Col. 1:13.
208. John 8:36.
209. Heb. 2:8; 1 Thes. 3:5; James 4:8.
210. Gal. 5:1.

Spirit empowers each believer to make wise choices and enables each one to follow through unto victory. "You *are* a chosen generation, a royal priesthood, a holy nation, His own special people, that you may proclaim the praises of Him who called you out of darkness into His marvelous light; who once *were* not a people but *are* now the people of God...."[211] Through the redemptive ministry of Jesus and the gift of the Holy Spirit, God has established a new nation among the nations of the world, that is the Church, the body of Jesus Christ. It is through the Church that God reveals Himself and attracts sinners to salvation and perpetuates His holy presence among every nation of this world.

John the Baptist saw "Jesus coming toward him and said, 'Behold! The Lamb of God who takes away the sin of the world!'"[212] Listed below are seven aspects regarding the Passover meal that foreshadow Jesus Christ our Passover Lamb.

1. The Passover marked the beginning of months for the nation of Israel.[213] Receiving Jesus Christ as the Passover Lamb of God by faith marks the beginning of months or the beginning of a new life for a believer.[214] The former life in bondage to sin is blotted out to be remembered no more. "Old things have passed away, and behold, all things have become new."[215]

2. "Your lamb shall be without blemish." Jesus proceeded through a series of trials concluding with Pilate stating, "I have found no fault

---

211. 1 Peter 2:9-10.
212. John 1:29.
213. Exod. 12:2.
214. John 3:5; 2 Cor. 5:17.
215. 2 Cor. 5:17.

in this Man."[216] Truly, Jesus was the "Lamb without blemish and without spot."[217]

3. "A male of the first year."[218] Jesus the Man is our Passover. "For if by the one man's offense many died, much more the grace of God and the gift by the grace of the one Man, Jesus Christ, abounded to many."[219] Jesus was in the strength of His life, about 33 years old when He was crucified. At the cross Jesus could say, "He weakened My strength in the way; He shortened My days."[220]

4. The Passover lamb was to be killed between the evenings.[221] Jesus was on the cross from 9 a.m. until 3 p.m., meaning He was crucified between the evenings.[222] An exact fulfillment of the Old Testament type by the reality of Jesus' crucifixion.

5. The blood of the lamb was to be put on the two doorposts and the lintel of the houses as a sign. And when the Lord sees the blood, He would Passover them and protect them from the destroyer.[223] The blood applied made all in the household safe from the destroyer and liberated them from the bondage of the evil taskmaster. "In His death Jesus is the Lamb, but in His resurrection, He is the Door—the only entrance of the household of God, the Household of faith."[224]

6. The flesh of the Passover lamb was to be roasted in fire, eaten with unleavened bread, and bitter herbs in one night.[225] The Passover

216. Luke 23:14; John 18:38, 19:4-6.

217. 1 Peter 1:19.

218. Exod. 12:5.

219. Rom. 5:15.

220. Psa. 102:23.

221. Exod. 12:6 "at twilight" literally means "between the evenings".

222. Mark 15:25-33; Matt. 27:45; Luke 23:44.

223. Exod. 12:7, 13, 22.

224. John 10:7-9. Kevin J. Conner, *The Feasts of Israel* (Portland, OR: BT Publishing, 1980), 19.

225. Exod. 12:8-10.

Lamb was not to be boiled but roasted with fire and any portion not eaten that night was to be burned-up in fire. Although Jesus our Passover Lamb was without sin, as typified by the unleavened bread. He suffered and died on the cross as our substitute. Just before His death He declared "It is finished." In other words, His sinless life was consumed by the fire of God's wrath as our substitute. It was a bitter experience for Jesus.

7. Not a bone was to be broken.[226] As the day ended the Roman soldiers came and broke the legs of those crucified on each side of Jesus to quicken their death.[227] However, Jesus had already died, but to be sure "one of the soldiers pierced His side with a spear, and immediately blood and water came out."[228] Therefore, in exact fulfillment of the Old Testament type, not one of Jesus' bones were broken.

The implementation of the first Passover in Egypt was God working His redemptive plan through the Children of Israel in anticipation of the day when He would send His Son into the world to die on the cross. That first Passover was to be celebrated by the Old Testament family of God as a memorial of God's mighty hand of deliverance from Egyptian bondage and their birthday as a nation. However, it was only a shadow of the reality of the deliverance that Jesus Christ the Lamb of God would bring to New Testament believers and a new holy nation called the Church of Jesus Christ. "For indeed Christ, our Passover, was sacrificed for us."[229] Jesus redeemed us with His own blood and delivered us from the bondage of sin and the power of darkness.

---

226. Exod. 12:46.
227. John 19:31-33.
228. John 19:34.
229. 1 Cor. 5:7.

Jonah and the Great Fish:

The story of Jonah and his experience of three days and nights in the belly of a great fish may seem to be an unusual place to find a foreshadow of the cross. But the words of Jesus tie the two experiences together. Jesus said, "For as Jonah was three days and three nights in the belly of the great fish, so will the Son of Man be three days and three nights in the heart of the earth."[230] Some of today's enlightened persons, reject this story as a fable and others consider it with much skepticism. But R. C. Lenski makes these comments: "Jesus himself states that Jonah was in the belly (κοιλία, abdominal cavity) of the sea monster "for three days and three nights" (quoted from Jonah 1:17) exactly as the book of Jonah records."[231] Paul Mackrell states, "Although he does not realize it, Jonah is playing the lead role in a drama which will serve as a little cameo of Calvary."[232]

Jesus does not consider Jonah as a novel or side story, but a foreshadow of His own death and resurrection. After Jonah was swallowed by the great fish, he was preserved during those three days and nights, then ejected on the third day to complete his mission in Nineveh. His victory over that watery grave is a testimony to the work of our all-powerful God. Death does not have the last word, God does. Because of what Jesus accomplished for us through His death, burial, and resurrection, we as believers are to experience the working of that same resurrection power in our lives. "But if the Spirit of Him who raised Jesus from the dead dwells in you, He who raised

---

230. Matt. 12:39-41.

231. R. C. H. Lenski, *The Interpretation of St. Matthew's Gospel* (Minneapolis, MN: Augsburg Publishing House, 1961), 492.

232. Paul Mackrell, *Opening up Jonah*, Opening Up Commentary (Leominster: Day One Publications, 2007), 46–47.

Christ from the dead will also give life to your mortal bodies through His Spirit who dwells in you."[233]

There are other aspects of the Jonah narrative that deserve our consideration. After Jonah turned his back on his mission to Nineveh and boarded the ship to Tarshish, and "The Lord sent out a great wind on the sea, and there was a mighty tempest on the sea."[234] David Guzik states, "We often think of Jesus calming the waters, and He can do that. But He can also stir up the storm."[235]

The sailors were afraid that the ship would be broken apart and they cried out to their gods. But Jonah remained asleep in the lowest part of the ship. The captain awoke Jonah and commanded him to pray to his God. But the storm increased its intensity. So, they determined that it was no normal storm, and someone was responsible. So, they cast lots and the lot fell to Jonah. The sailors now became exceedingly afraid and asked, "What shall we do to you that the sea may be calm for us?"[236] Jonah told them to pick him up and throw him into the sea. Jonah said, "I know this great tempest is because of me."

There is a phenomenon that occurs many times when God permits the powers of darkness to seemingly prevail against His purposes—just as Jonah thought he was prevailing by heading to Tarshish. The physical and/or spiritual circumstances around that situation are characterized as a tempest or storm. It also happened as Jesus approached the cross. It was like a tempest or a psychological storm. "Jesus said to them, 'All of you will be made to stumble because of Me this night,' for it is written: 'I will strike the Shepherd, And the sheep

---

233. Rom. 8:11.

234. Jonah 1:4.

235. David Guzik, *Jonah*, David Guzik's Commentaries on the Bible (Santa Barbara, CA: David Guzik, 2000), Jon 1:4.

236. Jonah 1:10-16.

of the flock will be scattered.'"[237] And stumble they did: Judas committed suicide, Peter denied Jesus three times, others ran for their lives, and only John stayed in the proximity of Jesus. In a tempest one can become like a "silly dove,"[238] disoriented and prone to go in the wrong direction. Therefore, we must learn to hear the voice of the Holy Spirit. Jesus said, "When He, the Spirit of truth, has come, He will guide you into all truth; for He will not speak on His own *authority,* but whatever He hears He will speak; and He will tell you things to come."[239]

Death seemed certain to the sailors and their efforts to save themselves and the ship are inadequate. "So, they picked up Jonah and threw him into the sea, and the sea ceased from its raging."[240] They were reluctant to throw Jonah to what appeared to be his death. But, if Jonah dies, the sailors live. Although Jonah told them to throw him into the sea, he never took the initiative to jump to His own death. That would have been suicide. In a similar manner Jesus said regarding His life, "No one takes it from Me, but I lay it down of Myself. I have power to lay it down, and I have power to take it again. This command I have received from My Father."[241] However, Jesus did not extinguish His own life. Others took His life by nailing Him to the cross. And on the cross Jesus said, "Father forgive them, for they do not know what they do."[242] And just as Jonah was discharged from the belly of the great fish three days later, so Jesus was raised from the dead and walked out of His grave early in the morning of the third

---

237. Matt. 26:31.
238. Hosea 7:11.
239. John 16:13.
240. Jonah 1:15.
241. John 10:18.
242. Luke 23:34.

day. The resurrection of our bodies is a great hope of all believers. "If in this life only we have hope in Christ, we are of all men the most pitiable."[243]

Summary:

The cross was a place of execution and a symbol of death which seems contrary to the loving nature of God. But Jesus taught this principle; "Unless a grain of wheat falls into the ground and dies, it remains alone; but if it dies, it produces much grain."[244] Even though God is love and He loves all people, sin is a moral violation of His holiness, and His holiness demands justice. Arthur W. Pink states, "God could not sacrifice His holiness to His love."[245] According to the terms of the everlasting covenant you were chosen in Jesus, the Lamb slain before the foundation of the world.[246] The cross was in the redemptive purposes of God before the creation of the world and not a secondary plan for our salvation. Therefore, our heavenly Father painted prophetic pictures that foreshadowed the cross through the pages of the Old Testament in anticipation of the actual crucifixion of His Son as recorded in the Gospels.

Abraham offering up his son Isaac to the Lord was the first foreshadow of the cross discussed in this chapter. In a world hostile to God, Abraham believed God, and was willing to offer his son Isaac to the Lord on Mt. Moriah. Abraham's faith illustrates the willingness of a father to sacrifice the son of his love to fulfill God's redemptive purposes. This foreshadows God the Father's willingness to sacrifice

---

243. 1 Cor. 15:19.
244. John 12:24.
245. Arthur W. Pink, *The Atonement*, (Swengel, PA: Reiner Publications), 272.
246. Heb. 13:20-21.

His only begotten Son on the cross. As God provided a substitutionary ram to offer on the altar instead of Isaac, so God has offered His Son, Jesus, to die on the cross as our substitute. Isaac coming down off that altar and going home with his father foreshadows the resurrection of Jesus.[247] Jesus said, "I am the resurrection and the life. He who believes in Me, though he may die, he shall live."[248]

The second foreshadow of the cross discussed was the sacrifice of the Passover lamb on that fateful night in Egypt and their release from slavery foreshadows the liberty that New Testament Believers experience when they put their trust in Jesus Christ the "Lamb of God who takes away the sin of the world."[249] As the Children of Israel were slaves to the Egyptians, so each of us are slaves to sin. They needed a Redeemer and so do we. Jesus Christ is our Passover and through faith in Him the bondage to sin is broken and believers are free to worship God in the beauty of holiness. We are no longer slaves to sin and captives of the evil taskmaster, the devil. Jesus came to "set at liberty those who are oppressed."[250] "But now having been set free from sin, and having become slaves of God, you have your fruit to holiness, and the end, everlasting life."[251] Our security rest in our relationship with our Passover Lamb, Jesus Christ our Redeemer. He has paid the ransom price to set us free and is able to do exceedingly and abundantly above all we can ask or think according to the power that works in us as members of His body, the Church, a holy nation,

Jonah's experience of spending three days and three nights in the belly of the great fish and then being discharged from that grave

247. Heb. 11:17-19.
248. John 11:25.
249. John 1:29.
250. Luke 4:18b.
251. Rom. 6:22.

foreshadows the three days and nights Jesus spent in the grave and was resurrected on the third day. As Jonah willingly submitted himself to the hands of the sailors to throw him into a watery grave, so Jesus submitted Himself into the hands of those who crucified Him and placed His body in a grave. Jonah foreshadows the resurrection of Jesus Christ and His experience of being discharged from that great fish paints a prophetic picture to inspire faith in the victory that God has designed every believer over the fear of death. Jesus said, "I *am* He who lives, and was dead, and behold, I am alive forevermore. Amen. And I have the keys of Hades and of Death."[252]

This chapter has focused on the prophetic pictures painted throughout the Old Testament that foreshadow the cross of Jesus Christ. We have only discussed a few, but there are many. For example, all the Mosaic sacrifices were shadows that pointed forward to the reality of Jesus Christ and have their fulfillment in Him. Soon after Jesus died on the cross, the Temple was destroyed, and the Mosaic sacrificial offerings were discontinued as the Holy Spirit drew and continues to draw men and women to the resurrected Savior. In the next chapter we will discuss the cost of the cross.

---

252. Rev. 1:18.

CHAPTER 3

The Cost of the Cross

"The next day John saw Jesus coming toward him, and said, 'Behold! The Lamb of God who takes away the sin of the world!'" (John 1:29)

"But now having been set free from sin, and having become slaves of God, you have your fruit to holiness, and the end, everlasting life. For the wages of sin *is* death, but the gift of God *is* eternal life in Christ Jesus our Lord." (Romans 6:22-23)

THERE IS WITHIN THE heart of every individual an innate desire, even a longing, to be the recipient of the father's love, fellowship, and blessings. This is true in both the natural and the spiritual realms. But man is born a sinner, and sin is so multifaceted, insidious, and destructive that despite human longings and efforts, relationships break down and we find ourselves hurt, resentful, and separated from members of our natural family and alienated from God. Often, we blame others for our hurts and isolation. But the reality is that we personally share the blame and need someone to help us bridge the gap that separates us from the ones with whom our hearts long to be united. Building that bridge is what the crucifixion and resurrection of Jesus Christ is all about. The damage that sin has reeked must be paid for by someone who is both willing and able to fully pay our sin debt. Jesus paying our sin debt is the cost of the cross. It was through the cross that Jesus made atonement for us. Sin is a multifaceted problem, so also the atonement is a multifaceted solution to sin as will be discussed in this chapter.

The atonement Jesus made for us through His crucifixion and resurrection include resolving three broad facets to sin: First, sin is a moral violation of God's holiness, and that violation demands justice. Second, sin resulted in changing man's nature and introduced death into the human realm. And third, it was through sin that mankind forfeited his dominion over the earth to the devil and the devil became "the ruler of this world."[253] These three facets of sin are addressed in the Old Testament on the Day of Atonement. But before we turn to discuss the Day of Atonement Walter Elwell offers these insights.

> The expression *make atonement* is frequent in Exodus, Leviticus, and Numbers, but rare in the rest of the Bible. The basic idea, however, is widespread. The need for it arrives from the sinfulness of humankind, a truth made plain throughout Scripture but infrequent outside the Bible."[254]

The concept of atonement is expressed in the New Testament with such terms as redemption, propitiation, forgiveness, righteousness,

---

253. John 12:31b.

254. Walter A. Elwell, *Evangelical Dictionary of Theology: Second Edition* (Grand Rapids, MI: Baker Academic, 2001), 113.

reconciliation, born again, godliness, eternal life, seated in heavenly places, and others. You can easily see that our salvation is a many-sided experience made possible through the crucifixion and resurrection of Jesus. Through His death, burial and resurrection Jesus did for us what we could not do for ourselves. We will begin counting the cost of the cross by first looking at what was accomplished during the Old Testament Day of Atonement.

The Day of Atonement:

From the time of Adam's disobedience until God gave the Law to the Children of Israel at Mt. Sinai, "sin was in the world, but sin is not imputed when there is no law."[255] During "these times of ignorance God overlooked sin."[256] Also, during this same period there was the "phenomenon of sacrifice"[257] which included burnt offerings, peace offerings, and offerings of thanksgiving. But the sin offering, and trespass offering were not offered nor authorized by God until He had made a covenant with the Children of Israel and instituted the Levitical priesthood to mediate between Himself and the people. While at Mt. Sinai "the LORD spoke to Moses, saying, 'Speak to the children of Israel, and say to them: 'The feasts of the LORD, which you shall proclaim *to be* holy convocations, these *are* My feasts.'"[258] The Lord gave instructions for the celebration of the weekly Sabbaths, the Sabbath years, and seven feasts which were to be celebrated annually.

---

255. Rom. 5:12-13.

256. Acts 17:30.

257. Charles E. Hill, "Atonement in the Old and New Testaments" in *The Glory of the Atonement*, edited by Charles E. Hill and Frank A. James III (Downers Grove, IL: InterVarsity Press, 2004), 25.

258. Lev. 23:1.

All seven Feasts of the Lord are significant, but we will focus our attention on the Day of Atonement.

> "And the LORD spoke to Moses, saying: 'Also the tenth *day* of this seventh month *shall be* the Day of Atonement. It shall be a holy convocation for you; you shall afflict your souls, and offer an offering made by fire to the LORD. And you shall do no work on that same day, for it *is* the Day of Atonement, to make atonement for you before the LORD your God. For any person who is not afflicted *in soul* on that same day shall be cut off from his people. And any person who does any work on that same day, that person I will destroy from among his people. You shall do no manner of work; *it shall be* a statute forever throughout your generations in all your dwellings. It *shall be* to you a sabbath of *solemn* rest, and you shall afflict your souls; on the ninth *day* of the month at evening, from evening to evening, you shall celebrate your sabbath.'" (Lev. 23:26-32).

The more complete instructions and details regarding the Day of Atonement are found in Leviticus 16. The Book of Hebrews, chapters 8 through 10, provide the New Testament interpretation and application of the Old Covenant Day of Atonement. This feast was to be celebrated on the tenth day of the seventh month and was a one-day feast. It was to be a "holy convocation" and they were to "do no manner of work" on that day.[259] It was to be "a sabbath of solemn rest" and

---

259. Lev. 23:1 and 31.

the only feast in which the Children Israel were commanded to "afflict your souls."[260] That means it was a day of fasting. On that day the Children of Israel humbled themselves before the Lord in repentance and prayer as the high priest made the prescribed offerings for the cleansing from the defilements of sin.

A major issue at stake on the Day of Atonement was access into God's presence. God is Holy and sin separated man from God. But God in His love and mercy for mankind now revealed a way for man to once again come into His presence. And that way is spelled out through the rituals on the Day of Atonement. The Hebrew word for atonement is *"kipper,"* which basically means "to cover." Through the sacrifices offered, the sins of Israel were covered, but the hearts of sinners were not changed. Therefore, the same offerings had to be made year after year.

It was the only day of the year that the High Priest was permitted by God to enter behind the veil into the holy of holies. "And the LORD said to Moses: 'Tell Aaron your brother not to come at *just* any time into the Holy *Place* inside the veil, before the mercy seat which *is* on the ark, lest he die; for I will appear in the cloud above the mercy seat.'"[261] Remember that Aaron's two sons had in the recent past carelessly gone in before the Lord and they died on the spot.[262] Hence, it is with the fear of the Lord that Aaron fulfilled the responsibilities of the High Priest on that solemn occasion.

On the Day of Atonement Aaron was required to lay aside the High Priest "garments of glory and beauty"[263] and "put the holy linen tunic and the linen trousers on his body; he shall be girded with a linen

260. Lev. 16:31 and 23:27.
261. Lev. 16:2.
262. Lev. 10:1-2.
263. Exod. 28:1-6.

sash, and with the linen turban he shall be attired. These *are* holy garments. Therefore, he shall wash his body in water, and put them on."[264] These were basically under garments expressing the attitude of humility. On this occasion the High Priest is not representing God to the people but representing sinful people to God. This is a picture of our Savior who, "being in the form of God, did not consider it robbery to be equal with God, but made Himself of no reputation...."[265] Kevin Conner states, "The linen garments symbolize the righteous and sinless humanity with which Christ clothed Himself, while the garments of glory and beauty speak of the glory which He had with the Father before the world began."[266]

There were three distinct features regarding the ministry of the High Priest on the Day of Atonement. First, Aaron the High Priest, had to make an atonement for himself and his household. Second, he had to make atonement for the Children of Israel. And third, he had to make atonement for the Sanctuary.

First, Aaron was to serve alone in the Tabernacle on the Day of Atonement. The Lord instructed; "There shall be no man in the tabernacle of meeting when he goes in to make atonement in the Holy *Place*, until he comes out, that he may make atonement for himself, for his household, and for all the assembly of Israel."[267] The sacrificial animals were chosen. Aaron was to offer a young bull as a sin offering and a ram as a burnt offering for himself and His household.[268] As the High Priest, he would take off his garments of glory and beauty, wash himself in water and put on the linen garments as he prepared to

264. Lev. 16:4
265. Phil. 2:6-8.
266. Conner, *The Feasts*, 55.
267. Lev. 16:17
268. Lev. 16:3 and 6.

make atonement for himself and Israel. Aaron was to "take a censer full of burning coals of fire from the altar before the LORD, with his hands full of sweet incense beaten fine, and bring *it* inside the veil. And he shall put the incense on the fire before the LORD, that the cloud of incense may cover the mercy seat that *is* on the Testimony, lest he die."[269] "He shall take some of the blood of the bull and sprinkle *it* with his finger on the mercy seat on the east *side;* and before the mercy seat he shall sprinkle some of the blood with his finger seven times."[270] This was to make atonement for himself and his household. The sin offering of the young bull was to be taken outside the camp and entirely burned with fire.[271]

Second, after making atonement for himself and his household, the High Priest was to make an atonement for the Children of Israel.

> And he shall take from the congregation of the children of Israel two kids of the goats as a sin offering, and one ram as a burnt offering.... He shall take the two goats and present them before the LORD *at* the door of the tabernacle of meeting. Then Aaron shall cast lots for the two goats: one lot for the LORD and the other lot for the scapegoat. And Aaron shall bring the goat on which the LORD'S lot fell, and offer it *as* a sin offering. But the goat on which the lot fell to be the scapegoat shall be presented alive before the LORD, to make atonement upon it, *and* to let it go as the scapegoat into the wilderness.... Then he shall kill the goat of the sin offering, which *is* for the peo-

269. Lev. 16:12-13.
270. Lev. 16:14.
271. Lev. 16:27.

ple, bring its blood inside the veil, do with that blood as he did with the blood of the bull, and sprinkle it on the mercy seat and before the mercy seat. (Leviticus 16:5, 7-10, 15).

Aaron would take the blood shed by the Lord's goat in a basin, with a censer of hot coals and proceed behind the veil into the Holy of Holies. He would follow the same procedure as when he made the offering for himself and his household. He would put the incense on the burning coals in the censer which would form a fragrant cloud before the Lord, and then sprinkle the blood seven times before the ark. Seven throughout Scripture is the number of completion or perfection. In this way atonement was made for himself and for the Children of Israel. Remember, the wages of sin is death and without the shedding of blood there is no remission of sin.[272] The life of the flesh is in the blood, and God in His mercy accepted the blood of the sacrificial animals as man's substitute, looking forward to the day when the spotless Lamb of God, Jesus Christ, would lay His life down on the cross and atone for our sins once and for all.

Third, Aaron would follow the same procedure in making atonement for the Sanctuary.

> "So, he shall make atonement for the Holy *Place*, because of the uncleanness of the children of Israel, and because of their transgressions, for all their sins; and so he shall do for the tabernacle of meeting which remains among them in the midst of their uncleanness…. And he shall go out to the altar that

---

272. Lev. 17:11; Heb. 9:22.

is before the LORD, and make atonement for it, and shall take some of the blood of the bull and some of the blood of the goat and put it on the horns of the altar all around. Then he shall sprinkle some of the blood on it with his finger seven times, cleanse it, and consecrate it from the uncleanness of the children of Israel." (Leviticus 16:16, 18-19)

You may consider it unusual for inanimate objects needing to be cleansed from the stain of sin. But "the altar before the Lord" or "the golden altar of incense" with the horns upon that altar speak of strength, the strength of prayer and praise. Human priests had ministered daily upon the golden altar of incense in the Holy Place, and the brazen altar in the outer court. All those priests were defiled to some extent by sin. Hence, cleansing of defilement was required. Thus, blood was put on the horns of the altar, and blood was sprinkled seven times upon the altar. All three sections of the Tabernacle were cleansed. Blood was sprinkled before the ark and mercy seat in the Holy of Holies. Blood was put on the horns and sprinkled upon the golden altar of incense in the Holy Place. And the burnt offerings were consumed upon the brazen altar in the outer court. Thus, the Tabernacle or Sanctuary was cleansed from the defilement of sin until next year when this process of cleansing would need to be repeated.

Now we can turn our attention to the second goat, the scapegoat.

"But the goat on which the lot fell to be the scapegoat shall be presented alive before the LORD, to make atonement upon it, *and* to let it go as the scapegoat into the wilderness.... And when he has made an end of atoning for the Holy *Place*, the tabernacle of meeting, and the altar, he shall bring the live goat. Aaron shall lay both his hands on the head of the live goat, confess over it all the iniquities of the children of Israel, and all their transgressions, concerning all their sins, putting them on the head of the goat, and shall send *it* away into the wilderness by the hand of a suitable man. The goat shall bear on itself all their iniquities to an uninhabited land; and he shall release the goat in the wilderness." (Leviticus 16:10, 20-22)

There were two goats, and lots were cast. The lot fell on one goat as the "the Lord's goat," which was slain, and its blood sprinkled before the Lord to make an atonement for Israel. The second goat, the "scapegoat", was to be presented alive before the Lord.[273] After cleansing the Tabernacle, the High Priest would come out and lay his hands on the head of the scapegoat and confess the iniquities of the Children of Israel, all their transgressions, concerning all their sins. Then he "shall send *it* away into the wilderness by the hand of a suitable man. The goat shall bear on itself all their iniquities to an uninhabited land; and he shall release the goat in the wilderness."[274] It is my belief that the scapegoat symbolizes God's provision to remove our sins far from us to be remembered no more.

One thing more needs our attention. It was on the Day of Atonement in the fiftieth year that the shophar was blown to

---

273. Lev. 16:8-10, 20-22.
274. Lev. 16:21b-22

announce the Year of Jubilee and liberty was proclaimed throughout the Land of Israel.[275] The land was not to be sold permanently,
because it was the Lord's land.[276] And in the year of Jubilee if a family
had lost their property for whatever reason, it was returned to the
original family's possession.[277] All Jewish slaves were to be set free.[278]
It was a year of rest and celebration.[279] Kevin Conner states, "Jubilee
year was literally 'the time of shouting.'"[280] The year of Jubilee will
have its final fulfillment when Jesus returns and Israel repossesses all
of its territory and lives in liberty and prosperity under the Lordship
of Jesus Christ.

The effect of the Day of Atonement was the forgiveness of sin and
cleansing from the defilement of sin which was absolutely necessary
for God to dwell in their midst and bless them. The Hebrew word for
atonement is *"kapar"*, meaning "cover, i.e., tar over something in a
covering motion."[281] In other words the offerings made on the Day
of Atonement provided a temporary covering of sin in anticipation
of the day when the blood of Jesus would not only cover our sin to be
remembered no more, but also cleanse the conscience of the believer.

The High Priest was permitted to enter the holy of holies behind
the veil into God's presence only on the Day of Atonement. However,
after His death and resurrection Jesus entered the heavenly and
more perfect tabernacle, "not with the blood of goats and calves,
but with His own blood He entered the Most Holy Place once for all,

---

275. Lev. 25:9-10.

276. Lev. 25:23.

277. Lev. 25:10 and 23.

278. Lev. 25:39-41, 54-55.

279. Lev. 25:11-12.

280. Conner, *The Feasts*, 64.

281. James Swanson, *Dictionary of Biblical Languages with Semantic Domains : Hebrew (Old Testament)* (Oak Harbor: Logos Research Systems, Inc., 1997).

having obtained eternal redemption."[282] "Therefore, in all things He had to be made like *His* brethren, that He might be a merciful and faithful High Priest in things *pertaining* to God, to make propitiation for the sins of the people."[283] Propitiation means that as a result of Jesus' death on the cross, the wrath of God has been satisfied. Now the pathway is opened for the forgiveness of sins and the gift of righteousness is made available including reconciliation with God.[284] Plus we now have access to God's presence all day, every day. We are invited "to come boldly to the throne of Grace, that we may obtain mercy and grace to help in time of need."[285]

Following all the rituals performed by the High Priest on the Day of Atonement can be somewhat confusing. But do not let the activity distract you from the primary issue addressed on the Day of Atonement, which was the forgiveness of sins and access to God's presence. Sin had separated man from God since Adam's disobedience in the Garden of Eden. But, at Mt. Sinai God in His mercy revealed a pathway into His presence through the blood of sacrificial offerings made by the High Priest on the Day of Atonement. The sin of the High Priest and the Children of Israel was "covered" or "atoned" by the blood of bulls and goats. The High Priest, the sacrificial animals, and the blood that was shed, all were foreshadows of the person and the work of Jesus Christ accomplished through His crucifixion and resurrection. On the cross Jesus, who had never sinned, became sin, and shed His sinless blood for the remission of our sin. He made propitiation for sinners, meaning, He appeased or satisfied the wrath of God. God's wrath having been satisfied; reconciliation is

282. Heb. 9:12.
283. Heb. 2:17.
284. Rom. 5:10; Col. 1:19-23.
285. Heb. 4:16.

now made possible through forgiveness of sin. We will discuss this more fully in the chapters ahead. "Therefore, brethren, having boldness to enter the Holiest by the blood of Jesus, by a new and living way which He consecrated for us, through the veil, that is, His flesh, and *having* a High Priest over the house of God."[286] Andrew Murray states, "The new and living way is not only the way for entering in, but the way for a daily walk, entering ever deeper into God's love and will."[287]

God chose you in Christ before the foundation of the world.[288] This clearly reveals that God had our salvation in His heart even before Adam's sin. Therefore, God in His love and wisdom is expressed in the Old Testament redemptive ceremonies that foreshadow the cross. The Day of Atonement is a prophetic picture that illustrates many aspects of the reality accomplished by Jesus through His crucifixion and resurrection.

The Lamb of God:

The New Testament opens with John the Baptist preparing the way for the Lord. When John saw Jesus coming toward him, he declared, "Behold! The Lamb of God who takes away the sin of the world."[289] After Jesus was baptized in the Jordan River by John and the Holy Spirit descended and abided upon Him, He was led by the Spirit into the Wilderness to be tempted by the devil. Having overcome those temptations, He returned from that wilderness "in the

---

286. Heb. 10:19–21.
287. Andrew Murray, *The Holiest of All* (New Kensington, PA: Whitaker House, 1996), 364.
288. Eph. 1:4.
289. John 1:29.

power of the Holy Spirit."[290] Jesus proceeded to minister powerfully, but He was about halfway through His earthly ministry before He told His disciples "that He must go to Jerusalem, and suffer many things from the elders and chief priests and scribes, and be killed, and be raised the third day."[291] His disciples did not understand His mission because they were blinded by their desire for Him to set up an earthly kingdom and deliver them from the Roman domination. They did not comprehend His mission "to seek and save the lost."[292] From His youth Jesus understood His Father's business included the sacrifice of His life on the cross. At a point following Jesus' entry into Jerusalem on what we call Palm Sunday, and just a day before the cross, the Apostle John records Jesus saying: "Now My soul is troubled, and what shall I say? 'Father, save Me from this hour'? But for this purpose I came to this hour."[293]

For Jesus to qualify as "the Lamb of God to take away the sin of the world," He must be without any blemish of sin.[294] After His arrest in the Garden of Gethsemane, He was led through a series of five trials. "They led Him away to Annas first, for he was the father-in-law of Caiaphas who was high priest that year."[295]

> The high priest then asked Jesus about His disciples and His doctrine. Jesus answered him, 'I spoke openly to the world. I always taught in synagogues and in the temple, where the Jews always meet, and in secret I have said nothing. Why do you ask Me? Ask

290. Luke 4:14.
291. Matt. 16:21; Mark 8:31; Luke 9:22.
292. Luke 19:10.
293. John 12:27.
294. Exod. 12:5; 1 Peter 1:19.
295. John 18:13.

those who have heard Me what I said to them. Indeed, they know what I said.' And when He had said these things, one of the officers who stood by struck Jesus with the palm of his hand, saying, 'Do You answer the high priest like that?' Jesus answered him, 'If I have spoken evil, bear witness of the evil; but if well, why do you strike Me?' Then Annas sent Him bound to Caiaphas the high priest. (John 18:19-24).

Assembled with "Caiaphas the high priest, were the scribes and the elders."[296] At this trial Jesus kept silent and answered nothing.[297] After a barrage of false accusations the high priest asked Him, "Are You the Christ, the Son of the Blessed?" "Jesus said, 'I am. And you will see the Son of Man sitting at the right hand of the Power, and coming with the clouds of heaven.'"[298] Then Caiaphas, the high priest "tore his clothes and said, 'What further need do we have of witnesses? You have heard the blasphemy! What do you think?' And they all condemned Him to be deserving of death."[299] Then they treated Jesus cruelly. "Some began to spit on Him, and to blindfold Him, and to beat Him, and to say to Him, "Prophesy!" And the officers struck Him with the palms of their hands."[300] "Immediately, in the morning, the chief priests held a consultation with the elders and scribes and the whole council; and they bound Jesus, led *Him* away, and delivered *Him* to Pilate."[301]

---

296. Matt. 26:57; Mark 14:53; Luke 22:54.
297. Mark 14:61; Matt. 26:63.
298. Mark 14:62; Matt. 26:64.
299. Mark 14:63-64; Matt. 26:65-66.
300. Mark 16:65; Matt. 26:67-68; Luke 22:64-65.
301. Mark 15:1; Matt. 27:1; Luke 22:66-71.

The third trial was before Pilate at "the Praetorium, and it was early morning."[302] At this trial Jesus continued to remain silent in the face of many accusations. "Then Pilate asked Him, 'Are You the King of the Jews?' He answered and said to him, '*It is as* you say.'"[303] "'For this cause I was born, and for this cause I have come into the world, that I should bear witness to the truth. Everyone who is of the truth hears My voice.'"[304] Then Pilate asked, "What is truth?' And when he had said this, he went out again to the Jews, and said to them, 'I find no fault in Him at all.'"[305] The Jews continued and were more forceful saying, "He stirs up the people, teaching throughout all Judea, beginning from Galilee to this place."[306] "When Pilate heard of Galilee, he asked if the Man were a Galilean. And as soon as he knew that He belonged to Herod's jurisdiction, he sent Him to Herod, who was also in Jerusalem at that time."[307]

Herod Antipas, the Tetrarch, was very glad to talk with Jesus, hoping to see Him do some miracle. Herod questioned Jesus with many questions. However, Jesus again remained silent fulfilling the prophecy of Isaiah, "He was oppressed and He was afflicted, Yet He opened not His mouth; He was led as a lamb to the slaughter, And as a sheep before its shearers is silent, So He opened not His mouth."[308] Jesus' accusers brought charges against Him and vehemently accused Him. "Then Herod, with his men of war, treated Him with contempt and

302. John 18:28.
303. Mark 15:2; Matt. 27:11; Luke 23:3.
304. John 18:37.
305. John 18:38.
306. Luke 23:5.
307. Luke 23:6-7.
308. Isa. 53:7.

mocked *Him*, arrayed Him in a gorgeous robe, and sent Him back to Pilate."[309]

This is the fifth and final trial for Jesus before His crucifixion. Pilate called together the Jewish leaders and said to them:

> You have brought this Man to me, as one who mis-
> leads the people. And indeed, having examined *Him*
> in your presence, I have found no fault in this Man
> concerning those things of which you accuse Him;
> no, neither did Herod, for I sent you back to him; and
> indeed, nothing deserving of death has been done by
> Him. I will therefore chastise Him and release *Him*.
> (Luke 23:14-16).

Pilate's offer to release Jesus was not received by the Jews, but they cried out all the more, crucify Him! Crucify Him! So, Pilate took Jesus and scourged him. The soldiers put a crown of thorns on His head and put a purple robe on Him. The soldiers said, Hail King of the Jews and struck Him with their hands. "Pilate then went out again, and said to them, 'Behold, I am bringing Him out to you, that you may know that I find no fault in Him.'"[310] But they continued to demand His crucifixion. Pilate questioned Jesus further, but Jesus remained silent. Pilate said, "Are You not speaking to me? Do You not know that I have power to crucify You, and power to release You?' Jesus answered, 'You could have no power at all against Me unless it had been given you from above.'"[311] Pilate "knew that the chief priests

---

309. Luke 23:11.
310. John 19:4.
311. John 19:10-11.

had handed Him over because of envy."[312] He made another attempt to release Jesus, but to no avail. So, Pilate sat in the judgment seat and delivered Jesus to be crucified.[313] "He is despised and rejected by men, A Man of sorrows and acquainted with grief. And we hid, as it were, *our* faces from Him; He was despised, and we did not esteem Him.[314]

The five trials of Jesus didn't start until after His arrest in the Garden of Gethsemane which was probably about midnight, and He was on the cross by 9 A.M. that morning. All five trials took place over a matter of only a few hours. The first two trials were before Annas and then before Caiaphas and the Jewish council. These concluded by charging Jesus with "blasphemy", because Jesus said He was the Christ the Son of God.[315] We know that "blasphemy" was a false charge, because He was the Christ, the Son of God. In the trials before Herod and Pilate the verdict was "I find no fault in Him."[316] Pilate's primary concern was not "truth," as a matter of fact his own words reveal that he did not comprehend "Truth."[317] His concern was political, therefore, rather than decreeing what was morally right and releasing Jesus, he took "water and washed *his* hands before the multitude, saying, "I am innocent of the blood of this just Person. You see *to it.*"[318] Consequently, the undeniable conclusion meant that Jesus was the spotless Lamb of God qualified to take away the sin of the world![319] The point is that Jesus was sinless and qualified before

---

312. Mark 15:10.
313. John 19:13-16.
314. Isa. 53:3.
315. Mark 14:61-64.
316. Luke 23:4; John 18:38, 19:4, 19:6.
317. John 18:38.
318. Matt. 27:24.
319. John 1:29.

God to make an atonement for our sin. The cross was the altar upon which the "Lamb of God" was sacrificed. But "without the shedding of blood there is no remission" of sin.[320] "Surely He has borne our griefs and carried our sorrows; Yet we esteemed Him stricken, Smitten by God, and afflicted."[321]

The New Covenant:

During His earthly ministry Jesus served under the terms of the Old Covenant. But, just a few hours before the cross at the last supper, Jesus introduced the New Covenant. He took the cup saying, "this is My blood of the New Covenant, which is shed for many for the remission of sins."[322] Following the last supper and in the agony of the Garden of Gethsemane, Jesus prayed asking God, "If it is possible let this cup pass from Me; nevertheless not My will, but Your will be done."[323] In that prayer Jesus relinquished His will to the will of the Father, thus committing Himself to be the sacrificial substitute for you and for me. Earlier Jesus spoke about His life saying, "No one takes it from Me, but I lay it down of Myself. I have power to lay it down, and I have power to take it again. This command I have received from My Father."[324] Jesus dying on the cross was a part of the Everlasting Covenant between the members of the Godhead. Therefore, Isaiah prophesied, "Yet it pleased the LORD to bruise Him; He has put *Him* to grief. When You make His soul an offering for sin, He shall see *His* seed, He shall prolong *His* days, and the pleasure of

---

320. Heb. 9:22.
321. Isa. 53:4.
322. Matt. 26:28.
323. Matt. 26:39; Mark 14:36; Luke 22:42; 1 Cor. 11:25.
324. John 10:18.

the LORD shall prosper in His hand."[325] In other words, the cost of the cross was determined in the Godhead before the foundation of the world and was no surprise to Jesus.

Jesus was on the cross for six hours, from 9 A.M. until 3 P.M.[326] While hanging naked before the world, and suffering the pain, guilt, shame, and judgment of God's wrath upon sin in our place, Jesus said, "Father forgive them for they do not know what they do."[327]

> Now it was about the sixth hour, and there was darkness over all the earth until the ninth hour. Then the sun was darkened, and the veil of the temple was torn in two. And when Jesus had cried out with a loud voice, He said, "Father, *'into Your hands I commit My spirit.'* " Having said this, He breathed His last. (Luke 23:44-46).

The veil in the Temple that partitioned the Holy of Holies from the Holy Place was torn in half from the top to the bottom.[328] This is a clear statement that the way into the Holy of Holies or into God's presence was now opened to all who believed on the Lord Jesus Christ. **This marks a major transition between the Old Covenant and the New Covenant.** Under the terms of the Old Covenant the High Priest only entered behind the veil into the Holy of Holies once a year on the Day of Atonement with incense and the blood of bulls and goats. But Jesus Christ, under the terms of the New Covenant, opened the way through the veil; "Not with the blood of goats and

---

325. Isa. 53:10.
326. Mark 15:25; Luke 23:44-46.
327. Luke 23:34.
328. Mark 15:38.

calves, but with His own blood He entered the Holy of Holies once for all, having obtained eternal redemption."[329] Under the Old Covenant the high priest made "atonement" for the sins that he had committed, then made an atonement for the sins of Israel, concluding by cleansing the tabernacle itself from defilements. Under the New Covenant, Jesus our High Priest, did not need to make an atonement for His sins because He was sinless. However, He also did much more that make atonement for New Testament believers; He made a propitiation for our sins which means He satisfied the wrath of God and made possible the cleansing of the conscience of believers. Jesus also, with His own blood cleansed the heavenly sanctuary.

> But Christ came *as* High Priest of the good things to come, with the greater and more perfect tabernacle not made with hands, that is, not of this creation. Not with the blood of goats and calves, but with His own blood He entered the Most Holy Place once for all, having obtained eternal redemption. (Hebrews 9:11-12).

Through bearing the sin of the world on the cross, Jesus became our High Priest after the order of Melchizedek and the "Mediator of a better covenant, which is established on better promises."[330]

> Therefore, brethren, having boldness to enter the Holiest by the blood of Jesus, by a new and living way which He consecrated for us, through the veil, that is, His flesh, and *having* a High Priest over the house

329. Heb. 9:12.
330. Heb. 6:20, 8:6.

of God let us draw near with a true heart in full assurance of faith, having our hearts sprinkled from
an evil conscience and our bodies washed with pure
water. (Hebrews 10:19-22).

These powerful truths will be discussed further in chapters ahead. Meanwhile, Joseph of Arimathea asked Pilate for permission to take the body of Jesus for burial, and Pilate granted him permission.[331] Jesus' body remained in that grave until early in the morning on the first day of the week. While it was still dark Mary Magdalene was the first to the tomb and to her surprise the stone had been rolled away and Jesus was not there. She ran to give the news to the Apostles. Peter and John responded by running to the tomb and affirming that Jesus was not there. It seems that Mary was then left alone outside the tomb and there she wept.

While Mary was weeping, the risen Savior revealed Himself to her. She apparently was so overjoyed to see Jesus that she attempted to clutch to Him. "Jesus said to her, 'Do not cling to Me, for I have not yet ascended to My Father; but go to My brethren and say to them, I am ascending to My Father and your Father, and *to* My God and your God.'"[332] Many scholars struggle with the timing of Jesus' ascension to the Father. But this much is clear; at some point after His resurrection Jesus ascended into heaven and sprinkled His own blood before the throne of the Father. Maybe it was after He talked with Mary in the garden or maybe it wasn't until He ascended into heaven forty days later. The Scripture does not make this timing clear, but the Scripture does make it clear that at a point following His

---

331. John 19:38-42.
332. John 20:17.

resurrection, He did ascend into heaven and cleansed the heavenly sanctuary. Jesus entered the heavenly Holy of Holies and sprinkled His own blood, making propitiation for our sin. Thus, it made mankind's forgiveness and reconciliation with God possible.

> For Christ has not entered the holy places made with hands, *which are* copies of the true, but into heaven itself, now to appear in the presence of God for us.... Not with the blood of goats and calves, but with His own blood He entered the Most Holy Place **once for all**, having obtained eternal redemption. (Hebrews 9:24 and 9:12: emphasis mine).

Andrew Murray states,

> Just as the cleansing of the Tabernacle was part of the dedicating of the first covenant, so the sprinkling the heavenly sanctuary, the cleansing of the heavens with blood of the new covenant, is our assurance that the sanctuary is open to us, and that the covenant is sure and will be fulfilled to us.[333]

It was later in the day of His resurrection that Jesus suddenly appeared to the Apostles while they were in a room with a shut door.[334] It seems with His resurrected body He simply passed through the wall into their midst. Also, there is no record of Jesus ever entering again the house in Capernaum that had served as His headquarters while ministering in the area of Galilee. Maybe it was possible that

---

333. Murray, *The Holiest of All*, 322.
334. John 20:19-20; Luke 24:36-40, Mark 16:14.

with His resurrected body He may have commuted between heaven and earth for those forty days before His final ascension. The Bible does not reveal where Jesus stayed during that period of time. A. W. Pink states, "That which the Savior would impress upon His beloved disciples was the fact that He had not left the grave simply to remain with them here on earth, but in order to enter heaven as their Representative and Forerunner."[335]

Some may ask, "Why would Jesus need to cleanse the sanctuary in heaven?" Sinful man had not had access to those holy precincts. One possible answer could be that Satan had had access to the presence of God according to the Book of Job and the Book of Zechariah.[336] Satan's iniquity could have defiled heaven.[337] George Smeaton states, "Sin was the ground of Satan's dominion, the sphere of his power, and the secret of his strength; and no sooner was the guilt lying on us extinguished, than his throne was undermined, as Jesus Himself said (John 12:31)."[338] This will also be discussed further in the chapters ahead.

SUMMARY:

Sin separates man from God his heavenly Father. Although sin multifaceted, God in His infinite wisdom and mercy has made every provision for overcoming the penalty, power, and presence of sin. Under the Old Covenant the Children of Israel celebrated the Day of Atonement by afflicting their souls or humbling their souls with

335. Arthur W. Pink, *Exposition of the Gospel of John,* 3 vol. complete and unabridged in 1 (Grand Rapids, MI: Zondervan Publishing House, 1973), 280.

336. Job 1:6-12; Zech. 3:1-2.

337. Eze. 29:15-18.

338. George Smeaton, *The Doctrine of the Atonement, as Taught by the Apostles* (Edinburgh: T&T Clark, 1870), 307.

prayer and fasting. God resist the proud but gives grace to the humble. God's grace was manifest on the Day of Atonement as the High Priest was permitted to go behind the veil and sprinkle the sacrificial blood before the mercy seat to cover his sin, cover the sins of Israel and cleanse the sanctuary from sins defilement. The High Priest did this year after year. This provision bridged the gap temporarily between God and man.

During Jesus' life He was "in all points tempted as we are, yet without sin."[339] Before His crucifixion Jesus suffered through five different trials and the final verdict was "I find no fault with this man."[340] Jesus qualified as the spotless Lamb of God to take away the sin of the world. Further, God is holy, and sin is a moral violation of His holiness and demands justice. Therefore, the wages of sin is death. In eternity past, before the foundation of the world Jesus agreed to bare the sin of mankind. At the last supper Jesus introduced the New Covenant and while in prayer in the Garden of Gethsemane He surrendered His will to the purposes of God. Thus, He agreed to take your place and my place on the cross as our sinless substitute. And on the cross, God "made Him who knew no sin *to be* sin for us, that we might become the righteousness of God in Him."[341]

Because Jesus was without any stain of sin it was not possible for the grave to hold Him.[342] Because of His resurrection, the devil no longer has dominion over you and me. Neither does sin have dominion over us. Because "once at the end of the ages, He has appeared to put away sin by the sacrifice of Himself."[343] "Brethren, having bold-

---

339. Heb. 4:15.
340. Luke 23:4; John18:38, 19:4, 19:6.
341. 2 Cor. 5:21.
342. Acts 2:24.
343. Heb. 9:26.

ness to enter the Holiest by the blood of Jesus, by a new and living way which He consecrated for us, through the veil, that is, His flesh, and *having* a High Priest over the house of God."[344]. At His resurrection Jesus "disarmed principalities and powers. He made a public spectacle of them, triumphing over them in it."[345]

God who is rich in mercy has "raised *us* up together, and made *us* sit together in the heavenly *places* in Christ Jesus, that in the ages to come He might show the exceeding riches of His grace in *His* kindness toward us in Christ Jesus."[346] And every believer in Jesus Christ is cleansed from the defilement of sin and liberated from the penalty of sin. "Let us therefore come boldly to the throne of grace, that we may obtain mercy and find grace to help in time of need."[347] All of these blessings now belong to you and me as a result of the price that Jesus was willing to pay for our salvation. In other words, the cost of the cross was the sacrifice of God's only begotten Son, because the Father so loved us and was willing and able to pay the price for our eternal relationship with Him as His sons and daughters. Therefore, sin, death, and Satan no longer have dominion over those who "confess with your mouth the Lord Jesus and believe in your heart that God has raised Him from the dead, you will be saved." In the next chapter we will discuss the cross and God's acts of grace.

---

344. Heb. 10:19-21.
345. Col. 2:15.
346. Eph. 2:6-7.
347. Heb. 4:16.

The Cross and Acts of Grace

"For the life of the flesh *is* in the blood, and I have given it to you upon the altar to make atonement for your souls; for it *is* the blood *that* makes atonement for the soul." (Leviticus 17:11)

"Help us, O God of our salvation, For the glory of Your name; And deliver us, and provide atonement for our sins, For Your name's sake!" (Psalm 79:9)

THE QUESTION ADDRESSED IN this chapter is "How can God be just and the justifier of the unjust?"[348] Or "How can God maintain His perfect righteousness and be reconciled with sinners?" The root of unrighteousness is sin and sin is a multifaceted problem that mankind alone is unable to resolve. But God in His infinite wisdom has provided a multifaceted solution for sin, and that is through the atonement. Understanding the many facets of the atonement helps to explain what was accomplished by Jesus pouring out His life on the cross. The crucifixion of Jesus was a demonstration not only of the love of God for sinners, but also reveals how repugnant sin is to God. Sin and/or unrighteousness provokes God's wrath.[349] In other

---

348. Rom. 3:26.
349. Rom. 1:18.

words, the righteousness of the cross reveals both the goodness of God's grace and the severity of God's wrath.[350] This chapter will focus on the atonement as it makes possible the release of the goodness of God's grace.

The Oxford Dictionary of the Christian Church defines "atonement" as "man's reconciliation with God through the sacrificial death of Christ."[351] This definition is concise and packed with theological meaning. That same dictionary also states, "... there has never been any official formulation in orthodox Christianity of the mystery of the Lord's redemptive work...."[352] Throughout church history the cross of Jesus and the atonement have been essential pillars to Christian faith. The Apostle Paul declared, "For I determined not to know anything among you except Jesus Christ and Him crucified."[353] But the Church has never worked out a concise doctrine of the atonement, such as the fourth century church fathers hammered out regarding the triune nature of God. It is not our purpose to try to formulate an acceptable doctrine of the atonement. Our purpose is to shed light on the many facets of the atonement and magnify the grace of God; while contributing to a better understanding of the wisdom of the cross of Christ.

The great turning point in redemptive history occurred at the Last Supper when Jesus took the cup and said, "This is the cup of the new covenant in My blood."[354] The new covenant had been prophesied six hundred years earlier by Jeremiah; "But this *is* the covenant that

---

350. Rom. 11:22.

351. F. L. Cross and Elizabeth A. Livingstone, eds., *The Oxford Dictionary of the Christian Church* (Oxford, New York: Oxford University Press, 2005), 124.

352. Ibid., 125.

353. 1 Cor. 2:2.

354. 1 Cor. 11:26.

I will make with the house of Israel after those days, says the LORD: I will put My law in their minds, and write it on their hearts; and I will be their God, and they shall be My people."[355] "I will be their God, and they shall be My people" is the essence or heart of God's covenant with all who will believe in the Lord Jesus Christ. Michael Horton states, "a covenant is a relationship of "oaths and bonds" and involves mutual, though not necessarily equal, commitments."[356]

Although our culture has developed an erroneous emphasis on personal rights, the new covenant is not about personal rights. The New Covenant is all about God's solution for sin and His reconciliation with sinners like you and me. The new covenant is a holy God establishing His non-negotiable terms for a personal relationship with all who would believe in Jesus Christ as their Savior. God defines the terms of this new covenant in the document which we know as the New Testament. *New International Dictionary of New Testament Theology* discussing the Greek word for covenant, *"diathēkē,* suggests that the covenant was no longer an agreement between two parties with equal rights. It came about as an exclusively divine action, which men can only accept in the form in which it is given to them."[357]

The New Covenant has three major components: (1) The words of the covenant are the words of our New Testament. (2) The blood of the covenant is the blood shed by the Lord Jesus on the cross, and (3) the seal of the new covenant is the gift of the person of the Holy Spirit to live in our hearts.[358] The words of the new covenant are more

355. Jer. 31:33; Heb. 8:10.

356. Michael Horton, *Introducing Covenant Theology* (Grand Rapids, MI: Baker Books, 2006), 10.

357. J. Guhrt, "Covenant, Guarantee, Mediator," ed. Lothar Coenen, Erich Beyreuther, and Hans Bietenhard, *New International Dictionary of New Testament Theology* (Grand Rapids, MI: Zondervan Publishing House, 1986), 368.

358. Eph. 1:13.

than a philosophical or historical presentation. The words of the New Testament do make us wise and record redemptive history. But they are more than simply wisdom and history; they are gracious words of Truth and Life.[359] The shed blood of Jesus is the blood of the new covenant that makes an atonement for our sin because His blood was without the stain of sin.[360] And the Holy Spirit seals our covenant with God and guarantees our eternal inheritance according to the terms of the New Testament.[361]

The Scripture declares two powerful realities regarding the shedding of blood and the atonement. First, "For the life of the flesh *is* in the blood, and I have given it to you upon the altar to make atonement for your souls; for it *is* the blood *that* makes atonement for the soul."[362] And second, "According to the law almost all things are purified with blood, and without shedding of blood there is no remission."[363] Most of us have at some point ask, "Why is the shedding of blood necessary for making an atonement? Why can't we simply verbally negotiate a peace with God? First, because we are all sinners and "the wages of sin is death."[364] Death means to be separated from God, the source of life.[365] Second, for blood to make an atonement it must be without the stain of sin. Jesus was crucified between two other men. They shed their blood, but it was not acceptable to God for making atonement for sin. Jesus was tempted at all points as all people are tempted, but He never sinned. So, His blood was without the stain of sin, making it

---

359. John 1:17; 6:63; 14:6; 17:17; 18:37.
360. Heb. 4:15.
361. Eph. 1:14.
362. Lev. 17:11.
363. Heb. 9:22.
364. Rom.3:23, 6:23; Isa. 59:2.
365. John 1:4.

acceptable to God for an atonement.[366] And finally, the Apostle Peter makes this affirming statement, "You were not redeemed with corruptible things, *like* silver or gold, from your aimless conduct *received by tradition from your fathers*, but with the precious blood of Christ, as of a lamb without blemish and without spot."[367]

As a result of sin, man is not only separated from God the source of life, but there is none seeking for God.[368] But God the Father was not willing to abandon His fallen and sinful children, but sent His only begotten Son to save them. The man, Jesus Christ, was uniquely qualified to be mankind's Savior as a result of His virgin birth and sinless character."[369] He, of His own volition, humbled Himself and made Himself of no reputation, serving His Father by first seeking the lost, and then, willingly laying His life down on the cross to make an atonement for their sin in order to reconcile repentant sinners to God. Through these efforts Jesus became the Mediator of the New Covenant. In other words, Jesus made the new covenant, prophesied, by Jeremiah a reality for you and me. H.W. Hoehner sighting Hebrews 8:6 states, "Christ as the mediator sacrificed his life in order to inaugurate the new covenant and thereby reconciled man to God."[370] The Apostle Paul states, "For *there is* one God and one Mediator between God and men, *the* Man Christ Jesus."[371] Jack Hayford speaking of Jesus' role as a Mediator says, "Jesus accomplishing salvation by

---

366. Heb. 4:15.

367. 1 Peter 1:18-19.

368. Rom. 3:11-12; Luke 19:10, 15:4-7.

369. John 10:11-14.

370. H. W. Hoehner, "Mediator" in, *Evangelical Dictionary of Theology: Second Edition*, Walter A. Elwell, ed. (Grand Rapids, MI: Baker Academic, 2001), 754.

371. 1 Tim 2:5.

His vicarious death (1 Tim. 2:5) and guaranteeing the terms of the new covenant (Heb. 8:6;9:15;12:24)."[372]

Jesus' vicarious death means that He suffered on the cross paying our penalty for sin and died in our place as our substitute. However, God raised Him up from the grave, "having loosed the pains of death, because it was not possible that He should be held by it,"[373] because He had never sinned. He suffered and died because "God made Him who knew no sin *to be* sin for us, that we might become the righteousness of God in Him."[374] Norman L. Geisler states, "Without Christ, the God-man, paying the price for our sins, God could not be just and yet also be the Justifier of the unjust, as Paul declared Him to be (Rom. 3:21–25)."[375]

It is crucial to emphasize that Jesus "has obtained a more excellent ministry, inasmuch as He is also Mediator of a better covenant, which was established on better promises."[376] The Biblical role of a mediator is to reconcile sinful man with our holy God, and that is the essence of what Jesus has accomplished through His death, burial, and resurrection. Norman L. Geisler adds, "Without the Just dying for the unjust, God's justice would not be satisfied, and without justice being appeased, God's mercy could not be released to declare the otherwise unjust sinners to be justified in His eyes...."[377] Millard J. Erickson continues, "Since this is true, it follows that the atonement, to accomplish for humanity what needed to be done, had to be

---

372. Jack W. Hayford, *The Hayford Bible Handbook* (Nashville, TE: Thomas Nelson, Inc., 1995), 713.

373. Acts 2:24.

374. 2 Cor. 5:21.

375. Norman L. Geisler, *Systematic Theology, Volume Three: Sin, Salvation* (Minneapolis, MN: Bethany House Publishers, 2004), 218.

376. Heb. 8:6.

377. Geisler, *Systematic Theology, Volume Three*, 218.

made by someone else on humanity's behalf."[378] May we never forget that the atonement originated in the heart of God because He loved us. John Murray states, "Love is not something that God may choose to be or choose not to be. He is love, and that necessarily, inherently, and eternally."[379] God was not obligated to provide a Savior or save any sinners. But "God so loved the world that He gave His only begotten Son, that whoever believes in Him should not perish but have everlasting life."[380]

So far in this chapter we have established that God sent His only begotten Son into the world to seek and to save the lost. Jesus ate and drank among sinners to lead them into being reconciled with God. But to complete the task of reconciliation, He had to abolish death and bring life and immortality into the reach of repentant sinners.[381] And this He did as our Mediator by making an atonement for our sin. As we stated earlier, "atonement" means, man's reconciliation with God through the sacrificial death of Christ. "Jesus fulfills what the Old Testament could grant only by way of anticipation. His death is consistently presented as an atoning sacrifice for sins."[382] George Eldon Ladd states, "While "atonement" is not a New Testament word, the idea that the death of Christ dealt with the problem of human sin and brought people into fellowship with God is one of the central ideas of the New Testament."[383]

378. Millard J. Erickson, *Christian Theology.*, 2nd ed. (Grand Rapids, MI: Baker Book House, 1998), 821.

379. John Murray, *Redemption Accomplished and Applied* (Grand Rapids, MI: Willian B. Eerdmans Publishing Company, 2015), 4.

380. John 3:16.

381. 2 Tim. 1:10.

382. R. W. Yarbrough, "Atonement," in *New Dictionary of Biblical Theology*, ed. T. Desmond Alexander and Brian S. Rosner, electronic ed. (Downers Grove, IL: InterVarsity Press, 2000), 391.

383. Ladd, *A Theology of the New Testament*, 464.

As sin is multifaceted, so of necessity the atonement is multi-faceted. A. W. Pink points out, "the importance of distinguishing between the work which Christ performed and the results which that work produced. The need for so doing is great if we are to obtain anything more than a confused view of it."[384] The New Testament presents "atonement" with a wide range of words and their cognates. John Murray states, "In dealing with the nature of the atonement it is well to try to discover some comprehensive category under which the various aspects of Biblical teaching may be subsumed."[385] All the many aspects of the atonement of sin converge upon Jesus and the shedding of His blood on the cross. Since we have not discovered any single term to express the many aspects of the atonement, we will discuss it under four separate categories as follows: (1) Acts of Grace, (2) Steps of Faith, (3) Places of Rest, and the (4) Hope of Glory.

"Acts of Grace" are foundational elements of the atonement which only the members of the Godhead initiate and execute. Some of these were executed by God before the foundation of the world. Man plays no part in the initiation or execution of these acts of grace even though each element is crucial to personal salvation. They are manifestations of a Father's wisdom and His passion to be in covenantal fellowship with His children. "Steps of Faith" include aspects of the atonement initiated by God's grace that in turn ignite faith in the hearts of individuals like you and me. Steps of faith results in us becoming participants with God in His acts of grace. "Places of Rest" originates in the atonement and is participated in through our personal relationship with Jesus Christ. Rest is a result of the

---

384. Pink, *The Atonement*, 186.
385. Murray, *Redemption Accomplished*, 14.

atonement, and we are charged to "be diligent to enter that rest."[386] Resting in Jesus Christ is a fortress of protection against anxiety and fear that seeks to undermine and destroy our trust in God. "The Hope of Glory" is the final result of the atonement in which believers presently participate through faith and the operational presence of the Holy Spirit but will enjoy for all eternity in full reality after the bodily resurrection. The following diagram will aid in facilitating this overall overall view of the atonement.

[handwritten: before the foundation of the world]

Jesus Christ the Son of God

[handwritten: Lamb of God]

Mediator of the New Covenant

[handwritten: The God Man]

The Cross and the Atonement

[handwritten: King of Glory]

Acts of Grace	Steps of Faith	Places of Rest	Hope of Glory
Chosen/Predestined	Conviction/Repentance	Covenant	Immortality
Propitiation/Expiation	Justified/Righteous	Peace/Joy	Inheritance
Book of Life/Hope	Forgiven/Reconciled/United	Access/Vision	Reign w/Christ
Redemption/Ransom	Regeneration/Sealed	Adoption	Glorious Light
Calling/Deliverance	Power/Authority	Liberty	New Jerusalem

[handwritten: Man is passive]

It is only through the death, burial, resurrection, and ascension of Jesus that salvation is made available to whosoever will believe on Him. Millard J. Erickson states,

> Our understanding of Christ's nature is crucial here…. Christ is both God and human. He is the eternal, preexistent, Second Person of the Trinity. He is God in the same sense and to the same degree as is the Father, a sense in which no other human has ever been or will ever be divine. To his deity he added hu-

[handwritten right margin: Romans Limited Q 1 in Christ; light of life 2:6-7; 4:1-2 vs 17; Gal. 6:14-6; Gal. 6:14-6; 1 peter 1:2-11]

---

386. Heb. 4:11.

manity. He did not give up his deity in any respect, but only the independent exercise of his divine attributes. In our understanding, Jesus' humanity means that his atoning death is applicable to human beings. Because Jesus was really one of us, he was able to redeem us.[387]

Part One: Acts of Grace

Grace is the operational power of God's presence that favors you and me. It means that God extends His love toward us without any merit on our part. That is why some define grace as "unmerited favor." But grace is more than unmerited favor, although that is included in grace. Grace is the unleashing of God's loving presence, rather than His wrath which we sinners deserve. His grace upon our hearts and lives initiates the possibility of the accomplishment of His glorious purposes of salvation. He unleashes His grace upon us even while we are still sinners, to the praise of the glory of His grace.[388] This extravagant gift of grace that brings salvation has appeared to all men and women.[389] We will now focus on particular acts of grace.

Chosen/Predestined:

Having stated that Jesus, the Son of God, is the unique God/man and the Mediator of the New Covenant, we will continue by discussing the first component of the atonement or acts of grace: chosen/predestined. Chosen includes the concept of you being selected by God. But we must understand that we were selected by God or chosen

---

387. Erickson, *Christian Theology*. 821-822.
388. Rom. 5:8; Eph. 1:6.
389. Titus 2:11.

"in Christ." God chose you and me because Christ alone made it possible for God to accept us. This clearly reveals that we did not do good works or become a good person and merit being chosen and predestined by God. Deserving to be chosen is out of the question because we were born sinners. "There is none that does good, no, not one."[390] The truth is that God the Father "chose you in Christ before the foundation of the world, that we should be holy and without blame before Him in love."[391] Jesus affirmed that you were chosen by stating, "You did not choose Me, but I chose you and appointed you...."[392]

Although Jesus loves us and grants us the status of friends with the privileges of intimate fellowship, He will forever and ever be our Master.[393] We are the bride of Christ, the Church, but He is and will always be the head of His Church.[394] Gordon Fee states, "The Son is the "head" of his body the church, which not only exists in him but also draws all necessary life from the "head" to which it is connected."[395] The fact that God the Father chose us in Christ and predestined us to adoption, positions you and me to be recipients of God's saving grace. "For by grace you have been saved through faith, and that not of yourselves; *it is* the gift of God, not of works, lest anyone should boast."[396] If the gift of God's grace is not suppressed in unbelief it will inspire or ignite saving faith in Jesus Christ.

---

390. Rom.3:12
391. Eph. 1:4
392. John 15:16.
393. John 13:16, 15:15, 20.
394. Col. 1:18; Eph. 5:23; 1 Cor. 11:3.
395. Gordon D. Fee, *Pauline Christology: An Exegetical-Theological Study* (Peabody, MA: Hendrickson Publications, Inc., 2007), 306.
396. Eph. 2:8-9.

God in eternity past not only chose us in Christ but also predestined us. Predestine means: "to determine or decree beforehand."[397] What God has predestined, man can reject or rebel against, because God created us in His image, providing us with the capacity to give and receive love. To give and receive love requires a free will because love cannot be coerced or forced. In eternity past God predestined you in two ways. First, God predestined you to be conformed to the image of His Son.[398] And second, God "predestined us to adoption as sons by Jesus Christ to Himself, according to the good pleasure of His will, to the praise of the glory of His grace, by which He has made us accepted in the Beloved."[399] Thus, it was never God's intention for you to be an orphan. The primary objective of an orphan is survival because an orphan has no available parents to protect and provide for him; neither does he have an inheritance. All of us begin life as orphans because we are born separated from our Creator by sin. But God in His compassions calls us to believe on Jesus Christ as our Lord and Savior. Thus, through faith in Jesus, God becomes a "Father to the fatherless."[400] And in Jesus Christ, God the Father has predestined you and me to enjoy all the protection and privileges of sonship![401] The ultimate goal of predestination includes: (1) your response to God calling you personally to be reconciled with Him through the shed blood of Jesus Christ. (2) To experience the new birth or regeneration by the Holy Spirit, who will empower you to be transformed into Christlike character. And (3) your adoption or placement as a royal son or daughter in God's glorious kingdom for eternity.

---

397. Zodhiates, *The Complete Word Study.*
398. Rom. 8:29.
399. Eph. 1:5-6.
400. Psa. 68:5.
401. Eph. 1:11.

Propitiation/Expiation:

The second aspect of the "Acts of Grace" is "propitiation/expiation." The New Testament concept of the atonement is expressed by the Greek word *"hilasterion"* which is interpreted "propitiation,"[402] designating Jesus as the "mercy seat" or the place where the blood of the sacrifice is sprinkled, and the holy wrath of God was appeased or satisfied. Further, "propitiation"[403] presents Jesus as the means of "expiation" or forgiveness. The complexity of the atonement and Greek word *"hilasterion"* with its cognates may seem challenging to grasp, but William D. Mounce assists us in gaining clarity through the following explanations:

> Jesus is represented in the NT as the priest who does the atonement sacrifice (*hilaskomai*), as the One who is himself the sacrifice of atonement (*hilasmos*), and as the place where atonement occurs (*hilastērion*). Everything we need for forgiveness, for the removal of God's anger, and for reconciliation with him can be found in Jesus.[404]

Propitiation, as the "mercy seat"[405] focuses on the concept of atonement satisfying or appeasing the wrath of God. The mercy seat is the lid placed upon the ark of the covenant into which the two tablets of the law were placed. The breaking of the law is punishable by death, but God, through His Son Jesus, has made the provision to

402. Heb. 9:5.

403. Rom. 3:25. 1 John 2:2, 4:10.

404. William D. Mounce, *Mounce's Complete Expository Dictionary of Old & New Testament Words* (Grand Rapids, MI: Zondervan, 2006), 46.

405. Heb. 9:5.

extend mercy instead of wrath. The breaking of the law is sin, and "the wages of sin is death."[406] Sin deeply offends God's holiness, provoking His wrath. Our sin against God or our neighbor imposes a moral debt upon us. This is why Jesus teaches us to pray, "Forgive us our debts as we forgive our debtors."[407] God's violated holiness demands reparation or payment for moral damages. Without such payment a sinner abides under the wrath of God. And God is the ultimate Judge of what is right and what is wrong. That is how heaven's scales of justice work.

When Adam sinned by disobeying God's command by eating of the fruit from the tree of the knowledge of good and evil,[408] his nature changed from innocence to that of being a guilty sinner. Then Adam passed his sin nature not only to his children, but on down the generations to you and me. We do not sin and then become sinners. No! We are born with a sin nature; therefore, we sin. We do not need to teach our children to sin, they sin because it is their inborn nature. As sinners we are all under the wrath of God. But "God so loved you and me that He sent His only begotten Son, that whoever believes on Him should not perish but have everlasting life."[409] We are morally bankrupt and completely unable to save ourselves from the wrath of God. And without the shedding of blood there is no remission of sin.[410] And God said, "For the life of the flesh *is* in the blood, and I have given it to you upon the altar to make atonement for your souls; for it *is* the blood *that* makes atonement for the soul."[411]

---

406. Gen. 2:12; Ron. 6:23.
407. Matt. 6:12.
408. Gen. 2:17.
409. John 3:16.
410. Heb. 9:22.
411. Liev. 17:11.

God's only begotten Son lived among us and was tempted as we are tempted, but was absolutely sinless.[412] Yet He willingly submitted Himself to the cross and became sin, pouring out of His life's blood to pay the wages of our sin debt. "For God the Father made Him, Jesus the Son, who knew no sin *to be* sin for us, that we might become the righteousness of God in Him."[413] In other words, the sinless shed blood of Jesus our High Priest sprinkled on the mercy seat of heaven made an atonement for sin; thus, appeasing the wrath of God, and releasing the mercy of God to pay for our sin debt. Mercy always presupposes debt and expressed mercy pays the debt of another.

Jesus shed His life's blood on the cross, releasing God's mercy (*This is one reason for interpreting the word hilasterion as "mercy seat"*). "Who is a God like You, pardoning iniquity... because He delights in mercy. He will have compassion on us and will subdue our iniquities...."[414] Jesus on one occasion told the story of a Pharisee and a tax collector who both prayed. The tax collector humbly prayed, "God be merciful to me a sinner." And Jesus said, "This man went down to his house justified."[415] God's mercy makes deliverance from His wrath possible to all who would believe on Jesus Christ as their personal Savior. This is a crucial aspect of the atonement or propitiation and reveals the righteousness of the cross. The cross of Jesus Christ makes it clear that God does not simply overlook sin, but accepts the sinless blood sacrifice of Jesus as the atonement for our violations of His holiness. Therefore, it balances the books of justice, satisfies His holy wrath, and enables Him to be just and the justifier of the unjust.[416]

---

412. Heb. 9:14; 1 Peter 1:19; 2 Peter 3:14.
413. 2 Cor. 5:21.
414. Micah 7:18-19.
415. Luke 18:10-14.
416. Rom.3:25-26.

Ben Witherington III quotes Saint Bede stating, "In His humanity Christ pleads for our sins before the Father, but in His divinity, He has propitiated them for us with the Father.... Christ is the atonement not just for believer's sins, but for the sins of the whole world."[417] Propitiation is the Godward aspect of the atonement, rescuing all who will believe on Jesus Christ from God's wrath. But expiation is the manward aspect of the atonement focused on God's forgiveness. God's wrath being satisfied through the atoning blood of Jesus, He is now in the legal position to grant a personal pardon to each repentant sinner from the penalties of sin which is the essence of forgiveness. The propitiation made by the shed blood of Jesus makes possible the resolving of the hostility between God and man and opens the possibility of forgiveness and reconciliation. Witherington III further states,

> Sins do not need atoning for, if God does not need to be propitiated. They could simply be forgiven, and cleansing could come through forgiveness rather than through an atoning sacrifice.... For both propitiation and expiation are necessary to take care of the sin problem and reconcile God and humankind. And the marvel is that the Advocate is propitiator, expiator, and propitiation all in one.[418]

While on the cross Jesus said, "Father, forgive them, for they do not know what they are doing."[419] In other words, by asking the Father to forgive His executioners, Jesus was in reality tearing-up

---

417. Witherington III, *Biblical Theology*, 460.
418. Ibid.
419. Luke 23:34.

their "I-owe-you," releasing them from the moral charges against them, because of their injustice against His innocence. Charles Hill states, "Though God is a holy Creator and righteous Judge, He forgives transgressions! Consistently and emphatically the Bible teaches that forgiveness is due to God's mercy...."[420] It is through the precious blood of Jesus shed on the cross that the atonement makes the propitiation for sin and makes possible right standing with God and the offer of God's forgiveness to all who will repent and believe on Jesus Christ as Savior and Lord.[421]

Book of Life/Hope:

It may be surprising to some to know that God keeps records. In writing to the saints in Christ Jesus at Philippi, the Apostle Paul said, "I urge you also, true companion, help these women who labored with me in the gospel, with Clement also, and the rest of my fellow workers, whose names *are* in the Book of Life."[422] The Bible does not say a great deal about the Book of life. But it seems that possibly before time began and before you did anything right or wrong, God not only chose you in Christ, but also wrote your name in the Book of Life. The Lord instructed John to write these words to the Church of Sardis. "He who overcomes shall be clothed in white garments, and I will not blot out his name from the Book of Life; but I will confess his name before My Father and before His angels."[423] Before the Lord can blot a name out of the Book of Life, it must have been written there.

---

420. Hill, "Atonement in the Old and New Testaments" in *The Glory of the Atonement*, 23.

421. 1 Peter 1:18-19.

422. Phil. 4:3.

423. Rev. 3:5.

This author does not know anyone whose name has not been written in the Lamb's Book of Life.

In other words, it seems that the Lord wrote your name in the Book of Life before you were born, even though He knew you would be born a sinner. He then implemented a plan for your salvation, a plan for you to receive eternal life. If you reject God's plan of salvation, and refuse to accept His acts of grace, then He has no alternative but blot your name out of the Book of Life. This indicates the Book of Life has an especially important function on the great judgement day.

> Then I saw a great white throne and Him who sat on it, from whose face the earth and the heaven fled away. And there was found no place for them. And I saw the dead, small and great, standing before God, and books were opened. And another book was opened, which is *the Book* of Life. And the dead were judged according to their works, by the things which were written in the books. The sea gave up the dead who were in it, and Death and Hades delivered up the dead who were in them. And they were judged, each one according to his works. Then Death and Hades were cast into the lake of fire. This is the second death. And anyone not found written in the Book of Life was cast into the lake of fire. (Revelation 20:11-15).

The richness of having one's name written in the Book of Life is found in the reality that everyone written in the Book of Life has a hope beyond this world and the confident expectation of eternal life in the blessed holy City of God forever and forever![424] Our God is a "God of hope."[425] Hope always has to do with the future. Our best is not behind us in what some may call the "good old days." Remember, there was a time when you lived without God and without hope.[426] But because of the death, burial, resurrection, and ascension of Jesus, you now have hope. Hope is not a simple wish, but a covenantal reality made vividly clear through the resurrection and ascension of the Lord Jesus! The resurrection of Jesus is "the firstfruits, and afterward those who are Christ's at His coming." [427]Jesus said, "Because I live you shall live also."[428] Death no longer has the last word, because hope sees that "death is swallowed up in victory."[429]

Hope serves as an anchor for our souls that holds us firm and secure in the midst of life's storms.[430] Because there is a future worth holding on to and fighting to possess. Hope is the covenantal basis of faith, and without faith it is impossible to please God.[431] People without hope give up the good fight of faith and surrender to the powers of darkness. The Apostle Peter proclaims, "Blessed *be* the God and Father of our Lord Jesus Christ, who according to His abundant mercy has begotten us again to a living hope through the resurrection of Jesus Christ from the dead...."[432] Therefore, "Let us hold fast

---

424. Rev. 21:22-27.
425. Rom. 13:15.
426. Eph. 2:12.
427. 1 Cor. 15:23
428. John 14:19.
429. 1 Cor. 15:54.
430. Heb. 6:19.
431. Heb. 11:1, 6.
432. 1 Peter 1:3.

the confession of *our* hope without wavering, for He who promised *is* faithful."[433]

Redemption/Ransom:

All of us are born slaves to sin. Redemption and Ransom are very closely related concepts that deal with the legal aspects of breaking the bondage to sin. The term redemption is sometimes used in a broad sense as a synonym for our salvation. But for our purposes here, redemption indicates that salvation is accomplished through the payment of a ransom. The concept of ransom includes the price paid to set captives free from the bondage of slavery. "Do you not know that to whom you present yourselves slaves to obey, you are that one's slaves whom you obey, whether of sin *leading* to death, or of obedience *leading* to righteousness?"[434]

All of us were without the authority/power to achieve freedom from the slavery of sin. What we wanted to do we didn't do, and what we did not want to do that we did.[435] "For we know that the law is spiritual, but I am carnal, sold under sin."[436] When explaining the meaning of "sold under sin," David Abernathy states, one "is not fully under the control of his own will, but is subject to an alien power.... The flesh is the seller and sin is the buyer[437]" We are not first slaves to the devil. We are first slaves to sin and as such, we are under the

---

433. Heb. 10:23.

434. Rom. 6:16.

435. Rom. 7:18-19

436. Rom. 7:14.

437. David Abernathy, *An Exegetical Summary of Romans 1–8*, 2nd ed. (Dallas, TX: SIL International, 2008), 483.

sway of the wicked one.[438] When the sin problem is atoned for, then we have authority over the wicked one.[439]

The only way out of this bondage of sin is to die. Our death is accomplished through the act of repentance, whereby we take personal responsibility for our sin and renounce it, asking God for mercy and forgiveness, and committing our life to the Lordship of Jesus Christ. Your repentance acknowledges that you are not your own and your life is hidden with Christ in God.[440] Then you can proclaim, "I have been crucified with Christ; it is no longer I who live, but Christ lives in me; and the *life* which I now live in the flesh I live by faith in the Son of God, who loved me and gave Himself for me."[441]

Regarding the atonement, the ransom price paid is not a monetary transaction where the Lord pays someone a fee/ransom to liberate you and me from the slavery of sin. Rather, it refers to the cost of our liberation from the slavery and bondage of sin paid for by the shed blood of Jesus Christ on the cross. Jesus said, "For even the Son of Man did not come to be served, but to serve, and to give His life a ransom for many."[442] The Greek word for "ransom" is "*lytron*," meaning the price paid or the transaction made to obtain one's liberty. R. C. Lenski explains it as, "the ransom is the life, i.e., the life of Jesus given into death; the ransom is effected by the sacrifice of that life, by the shedding of Jesus' blood."[443] Therefore, the reality for every believer in Jesus Christ is that you are no longer a slave to sin. You are the redeemed/ransomed of the Lord; you are not your own, for you

438. 1 John 5:19.
439. Luke 10:19; Matt. 28:18.
440. 1 Cor. 6:20; Col. 3:3.
441. Gal. 2:20.
442. Mark 10:45.
443. R. C. H. Lenski, *The Interpretation of St. Mark's Gospel* (Minneapolis, MN: Augsburg Publishing House, 1961), 464.

were bought at a price; therefore, glorify God in your body and in your spirit, which are God's.[444]

Calling/Deliverance:

It is the Lord who calls us "out of darkness and into His marvelous light."[445] God's call is a summons to respond to His grace. The Apostle Paul states that God "has saved us and called *us* with a holy calling, not according to our works, but according to His own purpose and grace which was given to us in Christ Jesus before time began...."[446] There are two primary aspects to God's call. First, we are called out of darkness into His marvelous light and reconciled to our heavenly Father. If a person rejects God's grace by turning a deaf ear to the call to be reconciled with Him, they forfeit deliverance from the kingdom of darkness and subject themselves to the wrath of God. Second, we are called by our heavenly Father to a place of service in the body of Christ, the church.

The purpose of God's calling is to inspire faith in Jesus Christ who will deliver us from the bondage of sin. As Moses was instructing Israel how to explain to their children why they should celebrate the final plague that released them from their Egyptian bondage, he said, "It *is* the Passover sacrifice of the LORD, who passed over the houses of the children of Israel in Egypt when He struck the Egyptians and delivered our households. 'So the people bowed their heads and worshiped.'"[447] On several occasions Pharaoh had tried to coerce Moses into compromised positions regarding Israel's deliverance.

444. 1 Cor. 6:19-20.
445. 1 Peter 2:9.
446. 2 Tim. 1:9.
447. Exod. 12:27.

For example, he told Moses that only the men could go and worship God, leaving their families behind; but Moses, acting upon the word of the Lord, demanded the deliverance of their entire households from their Egyptian bondage.[448]

As God used Moses to deliver the children of Israel from their Egyptian bondage, so the Father uses Jesus Christ to deliver New Testament believers from the bondage of sin and the powers of darkness. "He has delivered us from the power of darkness and conveyed *us* into the kingdom of the Son of His love."[449] When we are born again, we are given a new life, we also become a citizen of the kingdom of God. We are no longer strangers and foreigners, but fellow citizens with the saints and members of the household of God.[450] As a result, believers are residents here on earth, but citizens of heaven. God has "raised *us* up together and made *us* sit together in the heavenly *places* in Christ Jesus, that in the ages to come He might show the exceeding riches of His grace in *His* kindness toward us in Christ Jesus."[451]

As Moses was leading the children of Israel from Mt. Sinai towards the promised land, there were those Israelites who wanted to return to Egypt rather than face the trials and battles entailed in possessing the promised provisions of God. So, it is with some who have been delivered from the bondage of sin and the powers of darkness. They may get discouraged because of the way.[452] But for those who have been delivered from slavery and then return to the bondage of their former slave master, it would be eternally disastrous.

---

448. Exod. 10:8-11.
449. Col. 1:13.
450. Eph. 2:19.
451. Eph. 2:6-7.
452. Num. 21:4.

For *it is* impossible for those who were once enlightened, and have tasted the heavenly gift, and have become partakers of the Holy Spirit, and have tasted the good word of God and the powers of the age to come, if they fall away, to renew them again to repentance, since they crucify again for themselves the Son of God, and put *Him* to an open shame. (Hebrews 6:4-6)

All people in their own strength are incapable of deliverance from sin and the powers of darkness. But God has made every provision for our deliverance from bondage and entrusts us with the royal privileges of His sons and daughters and citizenship in the kingdom of God. "Stand fast therefore in the liberty by which Christ has made us free, and do not be entangled again with a yoke of bondage."[453]

In eternity past God predestined our salvation and His call to be reconciled with Him is where eternity past intersects with our present time. Gordon Fee states, "God's call is an expression of His prior will."[454] God calls us or summons each of us first, to be reconciled with Him through Jesus Christ. If we respond to God's call in faith, He then delivers us from the powers of darkness and conveys us into the kingdom of the Son of His love.[455] And second, God calls us to a place of service. Born again believers are expected by God to be more than simply spectators. We are members of the body of Christ the Church, and each member must function according to his or her calling for the body to be healthy and grow into maturity. Everything

---

453. Gal. 5:1.

454. Gordon D. Fee, *The New Testament Commentary on the New Testament: The First Epistle to the Corinthians* (Grand Rapids, MI: Eerdmans Publishing, 1987), 105.

455. Col. 1:13.

one does, no matter how small or large, is eternally important if God calls one to that place of service. Oz Guinness includes both of God's calls with the following remarks: "Answering the call of our Creator is 'the ultimate why' for living, the highest source of purpose in human existence."[456]

Summary:

When we first observe the cruel execution of Jesus through His agonizing death on the cross, one may ask, "How can there be righteousness in the cross of Jesus?" First, Jesus was not crucified by chance or accident, but by the "determined purpose and foreknowledge of God."[457] Second, God's purpose was to make an atonement for sin through the sinless sacrifice of Jesus. This He did to release His mercy and saving grace upon all who would believe on the resurrected Son of God. "For He made Him who knew no sin *to be* sin for us, that we might become the righteousness of God in Him.[458]

Therefore, it is crucial to understand that because of Jesus' sinless life "it was not possible that He should be held by the grave."[459] In other words, "The strength of sin is the law"[460] and Jesus never once broke the law, but was the spotless Lamb of God.[461] Hence, the grave had no authority to hold Him captive. However, His life was required because God does not simply ignore sin, but through the righteous and vicarious sacrifice of Jesus Christ an atonement was

---

456. Oz Guinness, *The Call: Finding and Fulling the Central Purpose of Your life* (Nashville, TN: Word Publishers, 1998), 4.

457. Acts 2:23.

458. 2 Cor. 5:21.

459. Acts 2:24.

460. 1 Cor. 15:56.

461. 1 Peter 1:19.

made for our sin, and death was abolished. Through His crucifixion, burial, resurrection, and ascension, He not only atoned for sin and abolished death, but also became the Mediator of the new covenant. The new Covenant is God's roadmap into the saving grace of God that guides all people into a personal and eternal relationship with our heavenly Father.

Because of the multifaceted aspects of both sin and the atonement, we are discussing the atonement under four categories. The category discussed in this chapter is "Acts of Grace." Under "Acts of Grace" there are five subcategories which are the foundational elements of the atonement. Only the members of the Godhead can initiate and execute these five subcategories. Some of these were executed by God before the foundation of the world. The five subcategories are summarized as follows:

1. Chosen/Predestined – We were chosen by God in Christ before the foundation of the world, not because of our good works or character, but because God loves us. We were predestined by God to be justified and adopted, which means to be made righteous and placed as royal sons in the kingdom of God.

2. Propitiation/Expiation – Propitiation has to do with the satisfying or appeasement of God's wrath towards sinners. As Image Bearers, all of us are loved and cherished by God. But as sinners, we are under the wrath of God. Jesus' sacrifice on the cross as our substitute satisfied or appeased God's wrath so He could release His mercy toward sinners. Expiation is the aspect of the atonement that legally releases God's mercy to forgive repentant sinners of their sin debt. "In short, propitiation is directed toward the offended person, whereas expiation is concerned with nullifying the offensive act."[462]

3. Book of Life/Hope – Before time began, God wrote your name in the Book of Life. Rejection of God's grace will blot one's name out of the Book of Life. It seems the ultimate function of the Book of Life will be the reading of its contents on the great judgment day. The blessedness of having one's name in the Book of Life is found in the reality of life eternal in the glory of God. This is a yet future glory, and hope is always future. God is a God of hope because He is the One who gives us a hope and a future.

4. Redemption/Ransom – All of us are born slaves to sin. Redemption and Ransom are very closely related concepts, indicating that salvation includes redemption accomplished through the payment of a ransom. The shed blood of Jesus pays our sin debt and through repentance we renounce our past life as a sinner and bury our old man in the grave of water baptism. From that point we belong to God. We go forth in the power of a resurrected life as the redeemed of the Lord under the guidance of the Holy Spirit.

5. Calling/Deliverance - It is while we are still sinners in bondage to sin and the powers of darkness that God calls or summons you and me to be reconciled together with Him through Jesus Christ. When we respond in faith to God's call, He forgives our past sin and delivers us from the bondage of sin and conveys us into the kingdom of the Son of His love. And whom the "Son makes free is free indeed."[463]

The substance of the subcategories above is not found in our works or rights, but in the acts of God's grace. Through His righteous

462. G. H.-Link et al., "Ἱλάσκομαι," ed. Lothar Coenen, Erich Beyreuther, and Hans Bietenhard, *New International Dictionary of New Testament Theology* (Grand Rapids, MI: Zondervan Publishing House, 1986), 151.

463. John 8:36.

acts of grace, God is both just, and the justifier of all who believe on the Lord Jesus Christ.[464] The cross of Jesus demonstrates God's gracious love for you and me. It is through the power of the cross that God's grace is released upon sinners, and the blessedness of the atonement makes reconciliation between God and man possible. "You were not redeemed with corruptible things, *like* silver or gold, from your aimless conduct *received* by tradition from your fathers, but with the precious blood of Christ, as of a lamb without blemish and without spot."[465] The next chapter will discuss "Steps of Faith."

---

464. Rom. 3:26.
465. 1 Peter 1:18-19.

CHAPTER 5

The Cross and Steps of Faith

"Being justified freely by His grace through the redemption that is in Christ Jesus, whom God set forth *as* a propitiation by His blood, through faith, to demonstrate His righteousness, because in His forbearance God had passed over the sins that were previously committed, to demonstrate at the present time His righteousness, that He might be just and the justifier of the one who has faith in Jesus." (Romans 3:24-26)

"For by grace you have been saved through faith, and that not of yourselves; *it is* the gift of God, not of works, lest anyone should boast." (Ephesians 2:8-9)

MAY WE NEVER FORGET that our God is a relational God and for all eternity the Father, Son, and the Holy Spirit have existed together in complete harmony. Mankind being created in the image and the likeness of God means that we were created for community. Everyone knows that one of the worst punishments for a person to endure is to be isolated in solitary confinement. The tragedy is that sin alienates and isolates man from his heavenly Father and from other members of the human family. But through the wisdom of the cross God has provided an atonement for sin whereby man can be reconciled with God and with ones fellow man. However, to participate in God's plan of restoration one must act in faith according to the covenantal terms of God. This chapter outlines the steps of faith one must take to participate in the blessed joy of a restored relationship with God.

Under the terms of the Old Testament the High Priest entered the Holy of Holies once a year with blood of bulls and goats on the day of atonement and made an atonement for the sins of Israel. The High Priest repeated this ritual year after year. But under the terms of the New Testament Jesus Christ our High Priest "has not entered the Holy Places made with hands, which are copies of the true, but into heaven itself, now to appear in the presence of God for us."[466] "Not with the blood of goats and calves, but with His own blood He entered the Most Holy Place once for all, having obtained eternal redemption."[467] Jesus has made the complete and final atonement and propitiation for every person's freedom from the bondage of sin and guilt by the sacrifice of His sinless life.

It is helpful as we seek to understand the many aspects of the atonement, to discuss the different elements separately. However, in our experience of obtaining salvation some aspects of the atonement occur in such a fashion that they are almost indistinguishable from one another on a timeline. Because each element of the atonement is significant in its purpose and function, we are discussing them one after another in a linear style even though they may

---

466. Heb. 9:24.
467. Heb. 9:12.

occur simultaneously. We continue by focusing on how every person is privileged to participate by faith in the redemptive work of Jesus Christ.

Part Two: *Steps of Faith*

Because the atonement is multifaceted, we are discussing it under four separate categories. In the previous chapter we discussed the first category, "Acts of Grace". We now turn our attention to the second category, "Steps of Faith". Steps of faith include aspects of the atonement united by God's grace which in turn ignite faith in the hearts of individuals like you and me. Steps of faith are required by you and me to participate with God in what His acts of grace have already made available. As we discuss the steps of faith there will be some back and forth between what the Lord has done or is doing, and the necessary steps of faith that we, as believers, must take to participate in the atonement. In other words, in the acts of grace all the action was taken by the Lord, and we remain passive. But under the category of steps of faith we must no longer be passive because faith is required to participate with the Lord in the following aspects of the atonement.

Conviction/Repentance:

Conviction is a process whereby the Holy Spirit persuades an individual of their sinfulness, that is their spiritual blindness and alienation from God, and proves that eternal salvation is available through faith in Jesus Christ the Lord.[468] Many times the Holy Spirit initiates conviction of sin by leading one to become dissatisfied and then

468. Eph. 4:17-19.

convinced that something about life is out of order or wrong.[469] We often hear the phrase, "Something is broken". Things are not working out according to your plan, even though you may be working hard. It is like being on a journey and ending up on a dead-end street, or like banging and banging on a door until we force it open, only to find nothing inside. At some point you may become exhausted and feel trapped, trying again and again to succeed with your own plans for success in marriage or career or business and ending with less than what you had when you started. Or it may be that you are prospering, and things appear to be going great, but deep inside you feel empty, unfulfilled, and dissatisfied. The first phase of Holy Spirit conviction is becoming persuaded that something is wrong and there has got to be a better life. So, you search for answers. What you may not realize is that God loves you and is involved in your frustrations, emptiness, brokenness, and dissatisfactions. The Holy Spirit is concerned with all that you go through and wants to bring you to the knowledge of Truth. At first, you may be thinking that no one really knows what you're going through. But God knows every detail and He is involved. His name is Jehovah-Shammah, "THE LORD IS THERE"[470].

Your conviction may develop through the following process. You search for answers, you hear the gospel of Jesus Christ through a TV program, or you decide to attend a church service. Or a friend or co-worker may share with you their personal testimony about how Jesus has changed their life. Then upon hearing the gospel something inside your being flashes with the hope of new possibilities. If you stop blaming others for your problems and personally take responsibility for the circumstances you are facing with a sense of a brighter

---

469. John 16:7-8.
470. Ezek. 48:35.

future, hope is birthed in your soul.[471] This is the second phase of conviction. As you continue to ponder the hope of the gospel and consider that God has a plan for your life if you are willing to change. All the while the Holy Spirit fans the flame of your hope of deliverance from brokenness, emptiness, guilt, shame, while offering eternal life in heaven. Now faith is ignited in your soul, you move into the third phase in which you seek a possible relationship with Jesus Christ as Savior and Lord. But how can one enter such a relationship?

At this point you are now convicted and persuaded of brokenness and personal sinfulness, but hope has ignited faith sufficient for you to believe that God loves you and is calling you into a personal relationship with Him. The hope of our personal relationship with God inspires you to act in faith by repenting of your life as a Sinner. Repentance is the God-given opportunity for you to confess, I am a Sinner, and have the liberty to make a 180-degree change of mind away from a life of sin and towards a new life under the Lordship of Jesus Christ. Now take steps of faith by asking the Lord Jesus to have mercy upon you and come live in your heart and be your Savior and Lord. Because God chose you in Christ before the foundation of the world and your exercise of faith in Jesus Christ by humbling yourself in repentance and by asking God for mercy, you enter the on ramp to a new life in the Lord Jesus Christ.[472]

Justified/Righteous:

When you repent and believe on Jesus Christ there is a legal transaction that transpires in the courts of heaven whereby God declares

---

471. Heb. 11:1; Rom. 10:17.
472. John 1:12.

his verdict upon you, "not guilty". Because of your faith in Jesus Christ, God takes the righteousness of Jesus and applies it to your account. Just as "Abraham believed God, and it was counted unto him for righteousness."[473] You are no longer a sinner, you are declared righteous, that is justified. You as a believer are "the righteousness of God in the Lord Jesus."[474] "But to him who does not work but believes on him who justifies the ungodly, his faith is accounted for righteousness."[475] "Therefore, having been justified by faith we have peace with God through our Lord Jesus Christ, through whom also we have access by faith into this grace in which we stand, and rejoice in the hope of the glory of God."[476]

When discussing "justification" the focus is on righteousness, not by works, but righteousness by faith. This may be a confusing issue for some people because the Bible speaks about two kinds of righteousness. First, a believer receives the righteousness of Jesus to their personal account in heaven by faith. "The righteous shall live by faith."[477] "But to him who does not work but believes on him who justifies the ungodly, his faith is accounted for righteousness."[478] Second, because of your righteousness by faith, you are then to do works of righteousness. "If you know that He is righteous, you know that everyone who practices righteousness is born of Him."[479] You cannot be justified by your works, because our righteous works are

---

473. Rom. 4:3.
474. 2 Cor. 5:21.
475. Rom. 4:5.
476. Rom. 5:1
477. Rom. 1:17; Gal. 3:11; Heb. 10:38.
478. Rom. 4:5.
479. 1 John 2:29.

like filthy rags outside of Christ.[480] Justification is the result of righteousness by faith alone.

To be justified is to be in right standing before God according to His terms. "Righteousness shall be imputed to us who believe in him who raised up Jesus our Lord from the dead who was delivered up because of our offenses and was raised because of our justification."[481] According to George Eldon Ladd the righteousness that is imputed to our account as a result of our justification "is not ethical perfection; it is "sinlessness" in the sense that God no longer accounts sins against him or her (2 Corinthians 5:19). The righteous believer... is absolved of sin by God's verdict."[482] In other words a believer in Jesus Christ is declared righteous by God. Then that believer has the responsibility by the gracious gift of the Holy Spirit to live right, that is to produce the fruit of righteousness. "For you were once in darkness, but now you are the light of the Lord. Walk as children of light (for the fruit of the Spirit is in all goodness, righteousness, and truth), finding out what is acceptable to the Lord."[483]

Forgiven/Reconciled/United:

The Father requires the injustices perpetuated by man's sin against His Holiness to be satisfied before He can forgive sin and be reconciled with man. The amazing thing is that His love has provided that satisfaction through the vicarious sacrifice of His only begotten Son on the cross. "In this is love not that we love God, but that He loved us and sent His Son to be a propitiation (*atonement*) for our

---

480. Isa. 64:6.
481. Rom. 4:24-25.
482. Ladd, *A Theology of the New Testament*, 488.
483. Eph. 5:8-10.

sins."[484] (Emphasis mine). The issue is man's need for mercy, because mercy always assumed a debt, and man has a sin debt that he cannot possibly pay. But God delights in mercy.[485] So, He sent His Son to bear the punishment for sin which is death. In other words, Jesus took my place and your place on the cross and shed His sinless blood and sprinkled it on the mercy seat of heaven for the remission of our sin.[486] Even though God delights in mercy, His demand for justice forbids Him from extending mercy to sinners until atonement/propitiation had been made by the sinless blood of Jesus. After His resurrection, Jesus Christ went before His Father in heaven and sprinkled His blood on the mercy seat of heaven, and that legally released God to be merciful to sinners. God in His wisdom accomplished this atonement/propitiation without violating His Holiness or justice. God's love expressed through the death, burial, resurrection, and ascension of His only begotten Son made every provision to extend the gift of forgiveness and offer reconciliation to all who would place faith in the crucified, resurrected, and ascended Lord Jesus Christ.

Forgiveness is the key that opens the door of the debtor's prison and sets the prisoner free. While Jesus was on the cross suffering for our sins, He said, "Father forgive them, for they do not know what they do." Frank Damazio states,

> Forgiveness is mentioned 124 times in the Bible. The first time is in Genesis 50:17 when Joseph's brothers begged him, "please, forgive the trespass of the servants of the God of your father." The brothers had mocked Joseph, ridiculed him, and sold him into

484. 1 John 4:10.
485. Micah 7:18.
486. Matt. 26:28; Heb. 9:11-14.

slavery. Now they were begging for mercy. Joseph's response was one of true forgiveness. "Joseph said to them, 'do not be afraid, for am I in the place of God? But as for you, you meant evil against me; but God meant it for good, in order to bring it about as it is this day, to save many people alive.'" (Genesis 50:19-20).[487]

The Apostle John states, "If we confess our sins, He is faithful and just to forgive us our sins and to cleanse us from all unrighteousness."[488] When the Lord forgives us, our sin debt is marked, paid in full. That means that God will never use our past offenses against us, even in the final judgement. When we are forgiven, we are set free from the debt of sin to live unto righteousness. It is something like having someone pay off your home mortgage. No more mortgage payments and free to use your income whatever way you want!

Forgiveness is a prerequisite for reconciliation. Reconciliation means: the restoration of harmony and peace where there has been hostility, enmity, and alienation. Where man's sin is atoned for through faith in the resurrected Lord Jesus, that person is positioned to be reconciled with God and restored to divine harmony and favor. "And you, who once were alienated and enemies in your mind by wicked works, yet now He has reconciled in the body of His flesh through death, to present you holy, and blameless, and above reproach in His sight."[489]

---

487. Frank Damazio, *Forgiveness: Releasing the Power of Grace* (Portland, OR: City Christian Publishing, 2007), 8.

488. 1 John 1:9.

489. Col. 1:21-22.

Having been reconciled together with God through faith and the Lord Jesus Christ, we then affirm our faith and new life in Christ through water baptism. "For if we have been united together in the likeness of His death, certainly we shall also be in the likeness of His resurrection, knowing this, that our old man was crucified with Him, that the body of sin may be done away with, and that we should no longer be slaves to sin."[490] To be "united" with Christ means to be entwined with Him in a spiritual relationship like strands of hemp are twisted into a rope or as a branch is engrafted into a tree. "And you, being a wild olive tree were grafted in among them, and with them became a partaker of the root and the fatness of the olive tree. Remember that you do not support the root, but the root supports you.[491]

The emphasis is upon our being "united" with Jesus and a covenantal bond like that of a man and wife in the covenantal bond of marriage. Paul E. Billheimer states,

> This is not a mystical, philosophical, symbolic, allegorical, or institutional relationship but organic unity. To illustrate: the members of a board of directors of a corporation have a functional relationship with one another. But an arm or a leg or a foot has an organic relationship to the body because each member draws its life from the life of the body. Just so, the born-again believer has an organic relationship with Christ because His source of life is in Him. The Church is not merely an institution ruled over

---

490. Rom. 6:5-6.
491. Rom. 11:17-18.

by Christ as President, a Kingdom in which He is supreme authority, but an organism which is in vital connection with Him, having the source of its life in Him.[492]

Being reconciled with God through faith in Jesus Christ as our Lord and Savior unites believers in an organic relationship with God that transcends time extending through eternity. Following the Last Supper Jesus prayed; "I do not pray for these alone, but also for those who will believe in Me through their word; that they all may be one, as you, Father, are in Me, and I in You; that they also may be one in Us, that the world may believe that You sent Me."[493] We are graced to be forgiven, reconciled, and united with our heavenly Father through the Lord Jesus our Savior. Nothing can possibly separate us from the love of God.[494]

Regenerated/Sealed:

Before God breathed into Adam, he was first an inanimate lump of clay. But when God breathed into Adam's nostrils the breath of life, he became a living being.[495] In other words, Adam's entire being was filled with breath of the life of God. The Scripture does not say this, but it is my opinion that the breath of the life of God shone through Adam's flesh, clothing him with the glory of God so that he probably looked much like Jesus looked on the Mount of Transfiguration.

---

492. Paul E. Billheimer, *Destined for the Throne: How Spiritual Warfare Prepares the Bride of Christ for Her Eternal Destiny* (Bloomington, MN: Bethany House Publishers, 1996), 58.

493. John 17:20-21.

494. Rom. 8:38-39.

495. Gen. 2:7.

Remember that God is so glorious and majestic that no one can look at His face and live. Even Moses had to be hidden in the cleft of the rock.[496]

Adam then enjoyed intimate walks and talks with God without the need for a mediator. But when Adam disobeyed God by eating of the forbidden fruit, his eyes were opened and he realized that he was naked, meaning that his nature had changed. The curse of sin and death now infected his whole being, which means that his spirit, soul, and body were separated from God, the source of his life. He was then a walking dead man.[497] As a result of his disobedience, he was sent out of the Garden of Eden to work the land by the sweat of his brow, until he would die physically.

About 2,500 years later God met with Moses on Mount Sinai and gave him not only the Law, but also the pattern for the construction of the Tabernacle, so God could dwell in the midst of His covenant people. Although God came and dwelt in the Tabernacle of Moses, He remained behind the veil and only the High Priest was permitted to enter behind the veil and commune with God once a year on the Day of Atonement. The point being that God always desired fellowship with man, but remained distant until His Son Jesus could come and make an atonement for man's sin. And Jesus willingly laid His life down on the cross to atone for sin. Upon the atoning work of Jesus, the veil in the temple was torn into from the top to the bottom.[498] Forty days after Jesus' resurrection He ascended into heaven and was seated at the right hand of the Father.[499] Ten days later when the Day of Pentecost had fully come, Jesus poured out the promised gift of

496. Exod. 33:20-23.
497. 1 Tim. 5:6.
498. Matt. 27:51.
499. Mark 16:19; Heb. 10:12.

the Holy Spirit. And for the first time since the expulsion of Adam from the Garden of Eden, God made Himself available to dwell in the hearts of all who would believe on the Lord Jesus Christ.

Once a person takes steps of faith by repenting of sin and believing on Jesus Christ, God the Holy Spirit, that same Spirit that God breathed into Adam, comes to live in that person's heart. The Holy Spirit coming to live in a believer's heart is the essence of regeneration. J. Rodman Williams states, "Regeneration means essentially rebirth: it is *re*-generation. Hence, regeneration is being born again or anew."[500] Jesus said, "Do not marvel that I said to you, you must be born again."[501] "But as many as received Him, to them He gave the right to become children of God, to those who believe in His name: who were born, not of blood, nor of the will of the flesh, nor of the will of man, but of God."[502] W. E. Vine, Merrill F. Unger, and William White Jr. state,

> The new birth and "regeneration" do not represent successive stages in spiritual experience, they refer to the same event but view it in different aspects. The new birth stresses the communication of spiritual life in contrast to antecedent spiritual death; "regeneration" stresses the inception of a new state of things in contrast with the old.[503]

---

500. Williams, *Renewal Theology*, 35.

501. John 3:7.

502. John 1:12-13.

503. W. E. Vine, Merrill F. Unger, and William White Jr., *Vine's Complete Expository Dictionary of Old and New Testament Words* (Nashville, TN: T. Nelson, 1996), 517.

When the Holy Spirit comes into your heart, He brings with Him a new kind of life and seals your new life in Christ.[504] "Now He who establishes us with you in Christ and has anointed us is God, who also has sealed us and given us the spirit in our hearts as a guarantee."[505] Norman L. Geisler states, "The *source* of regeneration is God; The *results* of regeneration is sonship; The *means* of regeneration is the Holy Spirit; The *duration* of regeneration is eternal."[506] The situation even after you are regenerated and sealed by the Holy Spirit, is that you still live in the same body infected by sin and death. But on resurrection day all people whose names are written in the Lamb's Book of Life will be resurrected and the old body will be changed in a moment in a twinkling of an eye.[507] Our resurrected new body will be glorious and immortal. That is what the seal of the Holy Spirit guarantees.

Authority/Power:

For some believers, including authority and power in the wisdom of the cross may seem unusual. But we must keep in mind that darkness and evil never retreat on their own volition—those enemies must be forced to retreat. And the capacity to force evil and darkness in retreat was granted by Jesus through the cross.[508] It is through the wisdom of the cross that God condemned sin in the flesh and restores to believers in Jesus Christ, the dominion that Adam lost. In other words, our heavenly Father is not only restoring fellowship with His children, but through the death, burial, resurrection, and

---

504. 2 Cor. 5:17; Gal. 3:26-29.
505. 2 Cor.1:21-22.
506. Geisler, *Systemic Theology, Volume Three*, 225.
507. 1 Cor. 15:51-52.
508. 1 Cor. 2:4-10.

ascension of Jesus Christ the dominion given to Adam before sin is also being restored. This reality is foreshadowed in the ministry of the seventy disciples Jesus sent out prior to the cross. Upon their return from ministry, they reported the joy of their success to Jesus. He responded, "I saw Satan fall like lightning from heaven. Behold, I give you **authority** (*exousia*) to trample on serpents and scorpions, and over all of the **power** (*dynamis*) of the enemy, and nothing shall by any means hurt you."[509] (Emphasis mine). R. C. Lenski states,

> Because Satan fell thus in defeat before Jesus, therefore Jesus can bestow the spoils of victory upon his disciples. Not because Satan was thrown from heaven, but because Jesus had defeated him and thrown him out of his rule and dominion does He now say: "Lo, I have given you authority," etc., and the perfect tense implies that this gift is still in force. Authority, *exousia*, includes both the power and the right to exercise power... Satan, indeed, has power, but the Seventy have authority from Jesus "to trample or tread" on it, which means more than to defeat that power, it includes the scorning and the derision of that power and of "all" of it, and both the physical and the spiritual realm domain.[510]

All authority originates with our sovereign God, "For there is no authority except from God."[511] The wisdom of the cross reveals that

---

509. Luke 10:18-19.

510. R. C. H. Lenski, *The Interpretation of St. Luke's Gospel* (Minneapolis, MN: Augsburg Publishing House, 1961), 582-583.

511. Rom. 13:1.

Jesus won three victories. (1) Jesus won a legal victory over sin in the court of heaven. (2) He won a dynamic victory over the powers of the devil on the earth. And (3) He won a spiritual victory over the spirit of unbelief in the hearts of the disciples. Paul E. Billheimer states, "When Jesus was justified and made alive, adjudged and declared righteous in the Supreme Court of the universe, Satan the arch foe of God and man, was completely disarmed and dethroned.[512] As the Scriptures declare, "Having disarmed principalities and powers, He made a public spectacle of them, triumphing over them in it."[513] In other words through the death, burial, resurrection, and ascension of Jesus, sin was atoned, the devil's authority over mankind ended, and the Spirit of faith was released.[514] The Apostle prayed the following prayer for the Ephesians:

> Therefore I also, after I heard of your faith in the Lord Jesus and your love for all the Saints, do not cease to give thanks for you, making mention of you in my prayers: that the God of our Lord Jesus Christ, the Father of glory, may give you the spirit of wisdom and revelation in the knowledge of Him, the eyes of your understanding being enlightened; That you may know what is the hope of His calling, what are the riches of the glory of His inheritance in the saints, and what is the exceeding greatness of His power (*dunamis*) toward us who believe, according to the working of His mighty power (*kratos*) which He worked in Christ when He raised Him from the

512. Billheimer, *Destined for the Throne*, 87.
513. Col. 2:15.
514. Rom. 4:16.

dead and seated *Him* at His right hand in heavenly places, far above all principality and power (*exousia*) and might and dominion (*kyriotes* = *lordship*), and every name that is named, not only in this age but also in that which is to come. And He put all *things* under His feet and gave Him to be head over all things to the church, which is His body, the fullness of Him that fills all in all. (Ephesians 1:15-23; Emphasis mine).

The wisdom of the cross has also altered the fabric of this world, that out of its pollution and decay the Kingdom of God advances, and a vibrant church presses forward, which the gates of hell cannot prevail against. The advance of the Kingdom of God will continue until, "the kingdoms of this world have become *the kingdoms* of our God and of His Christ, and He shall reign forever and ever!"[515] Meanwhile the Church will proclaim the gospel of Jesus Christ as a witness to the wisdom of the cross and the Lordship of Jesus Christ to the end of the earth.[516] Following Jesus' death, burial, and resurrection, but prior to His ascension, He made five powerful statements to complete His earthly ministry.

First, on the evening of the day of His resurrection, Jesus appeared to His disciples behind closed doors and said to them, "'Peace be to you! As the Father has sent Me, I also send you.' And when He had said this, He breathed on them, and said to them, 'Receive the Holy Spirit. If you forgive the sins of any, they are

---

515. Rev. 11:15.
516. Acts 1:8.

forgiven them; if you retain the sins of any they are retained.'" (John 20:21-23).

Second, "He said to them, 'go into all the world and preach the gospel to every creature. He who believes and is baptized will be saved; but he who does not believe will be condemned. And these signs will follow those who believe: in My name they will cast out demons; they will speak with new tongues; they will take up serpents; and if they drink anything deadly, it will by no means hurt them; they will lay hands on the sick and they will recover. (Mark 16:15-18).

Third, Jesus came and spoke to them, saying, "All authority has been given to Me in heaven and on earth. Go therefore and make disciples of all nations, baptizing them in the name of the Father and of the Son and the Holy Spirit, teaching them to observe all things I have commanded you; and lo, I am with you always, *even* to the end of the age. Amen." (Matthew 28:18-20).

Fourth, "Then He said to them, 'Thus it is written, and thus it is was necessary for the Christ to suffer and to rise from the dead on the third day, and that repentance and remission of sin should be preached in His name to all nations, beginning at Jerusalem. And you are witness of these things. Behold, I send the Promise of My Father upon you; but tarry in the city of Jerusalem until you are endued with power from on high." (Luke 24:46-49).

Fifth, just before His ascension Jesus told His disciples, "'You shall receive power when the Holy Spirit has come upon you and you shall be witnesses to Me in Jerusalem, and in all Judea and Samaria, and to the end of the earth.' Now when He had spoken these things, while they watched, He was taken up, and a cloud received Him out of their sight." (Acts 1:8-9).

As stated above, Jesus said to His disciples, "All authority has been given to Me in heaven and on earth."[517] Paul King states, "There is an important principle here in understanding the interrelationship between authority and power. Power without authority is illegitimate; authority without power is inadequate."[518] All authority was given to Jesus and the timing of that gift follows His resurrection.[519] He does not abdicate or relinquish His authority to believers, rather He delegates His authority to them. Therefore, believers are stewards or administrators of delegated authority. Jesus said, "In My name you will cast out demons; they will speak with new tongues; they will take up serpents; and if they drink any deadly thing, it will by no means hurt them; they will lay hands on the sick, and they will recover."[520] In other words when the disciples speak in the "name Jesus" they are exercising His authority. He has now gone into heaven and is at the

517. Matt. 28:18.
518. Paul L. King, *Come Up Higher: Rediscovering the Throne Life: The Highest Christian Life for the 21st Century* (Tulsa, OK: One Seed Press, 2013), 139.
519. Matt. 28:18.
520. Mark 16:17-18.

right hand of God; angels, authorities, and powers have been made subject to Him.[521] Remember the seven sons of Sceva tried to cast demons out of a man and failed because they were not in relationship with Jesus Christ.[522]

In the evening of the day of His resurrection He appeared to His disciples and "breathed on them, and said to them, 'Receive the Holy Spirit.'"[523] It was on this occasion that I believe the disciples were born again or born of the Holy Spirit. Just before His ascension Jesus said to them, "But you shall receive power when the Holy Spirit has come upon you."[524] Jesus ascended to heaven and when the Day of Pentecost had fully come, He poured out the Holy Spirit as the Father had promised and the one-hundred-twenty in the upper room were filled with the Holy Spirit.[525]

Jesus was conceived in Mary's womb by the Holy Spirit. Therefore, isn't it correct to say that Jesus was born of the Holy Spirit? However, to our knowledge Jesus never performed any miracles until He was clothed upon by the Holy Spirit following His water baptism.[526] The Holy Spirit is a person of power. Jesus' first recorded miracle was turning water into wine at the wedding feast.[527] Shortly after His miracle of turning water to wine, Jesus ministered in His hometown of Nazareth. He went to the synagogue as it was His custom and He was handed the Book of Isaiah and He read the following:

---

521. 1 Peter 3:22
522. Acts 19:13-16.
523. John 20:22.
524. Acts 1:8.
525. Acts 2:3.
526. Luke 3:21-22.
527. John 2:5-11.

THE MESSAGE OF THE CROSS

*The Spirit of the Lord is upon Me because He has anoint-
ed Me to preach the gospel to the poor; He has sent Me to
heal the broken hearted, to proclaim liberty to the captives
and the recovery of sight to the blind, to set at liberty those
who are oppressed; To proclaim the acceptable year of the
LORD. (Luke 4: 18-19).*

Jesus continued his ministry with manifestations of many signs
and wonders. The point being that heaven's authority and power
combined in the life experience of every Spirit filled believer constitutes what Jesus described in the Scripture above as "anointed".
"Now He who establishes us with you in Christ and has anointed us
is God, who also has sealed us and given us the Spirit in our hearts
as a guarantee."[528] We as the body of Christ are not simply "do good-
ers" nor "philosophers". No! We are the sons and daughters of God,
purchased by the blood of Jesus and granted authority over the powers of darkness and empowered by the Holy Spirit to set the captives
free until Jesus returns! Our weapons are mighty to the pulling down
of strongholds and having done all we can do, stand, "praying always
with all power and supplication in the spirit, being watchful to this
end with all perseverance and supplication for all the saints."[529]

When we consider all that Jesus accomplished through His death,
burial, resurrection, and ascension we rejoice that sin no longer has
dominion over us.[530] But until the return of the Lord Jesus we still
struggle with sin in the flesh.[531] So it is with the forces of darkness
and evil. Jesus has gained for us complete victory over the powers of

---

528. 2 Cor. 1:21-22.
529. 2 Cor. 10:4; Eph. 6:18.
530. Rom. 6:14.
531. 1 John 1:7-9.

darkness and the devil. "We do not wrestle against flesh and blood, but against principalities, against powers, against rulers of darkness of this age, against spiritual host of wickedness in heavenly places.[532] Believers will continue to wrestle against sin and the powers of darkness until Jesus returns and we receive our glorified bodies, and the devil is cast into hell. The point is, if we keep the faith we will overcome death because death does not have the last word, Jesus does!

Summary:

It was at the cross that Jesus willingly laid down His life and made an atonement/propitiation for our sin. Atonement is an Old Testament word and propitiation is a New Testament word. In the Old Testament the Israelites celebrated the Day of Atonement, whereby year after year the High Priest went behind the veil into the Holy of Holies with blood of animals and incense. He then sprinkled the blood seven times on the mercy seat to make an atonement, a God ordained cover for the sins of Israel. Under the terms of the New Testament, Jesus our High Priest shed His sinless blood on the cross and entered heaven and sprinkled His own blood on the mercy seat in heaven to make a propitiation for our sin, thus satisfying or appeasing the wrath of God and making provision for forgiveness of man's sin once and for all. The "Steps of Faith" discussed in this chapter are the God given means whereby mankind can participate in God's great plan of salvation.

1. Conviction/Repentance – In this context conviction means to be persuaded/convinced by the Holy Spirit that something is wrong and God offers a better life. Holy Spirit conviction often begins with

---

532. Eph. 6:12.

dissatisfaction with the way things are or the way your life is not working out for you. That results in you seeking solutions for your dissatisfactions. One of the first solutions that many people turn to is to blame others for their situation. But that most often ends by adding to their frustration. Your search will sooner or later lead you to hear the gospel of Jesus Christ and realize that you have a sin problem. As you meditate on the gospel, the Holy Spirit will persuade you that God has a better plan for your life if you're willing to change. Now the hope of a brighter future ignites faith in your heart, and you begin to desire a relationship with Jesus Christ, but how does one enter a relationship with Him?

At this juncture the hope of personal relationship with Jesus Christ inspires you to act in faith by repenting of your sinful lifestyle, then turning away from sin and turning your life over to the Lordship of Jesus Christ. That 180-degree change of your mind turns you from a life of sin by asking the Lord to have mercy upon you and be your Savior—that is the essence of repentance. It is first a change of your mind and then a decision to ask Jesus to be the Lord of your life. A new life with Jesus is contingent upon being convicted by the Holy Spirit of sin and persuaded by Him to take steps of faith by asking Jesus for mercy and to be your Savior and Lord.

2. Justification/Righteousness – To be justified means that following your conviction by the Holy Spirit and taking steps of faith by repenting, a legal transaction transpires in the courts of heaven whereby God declares you righteous. Because you acted in faith by humbling yourself in repentance and asking for mercy, your heavenly Father forgives your sin and it is removed from you as far as the East is from the West. And then He applies the righteousness of Jesus to your personal account.[533] In other words, justification means right standing before God and He declares you righteous, because your faith is accounted to you for righteousness.[534]

3. Forgiven/Reconcile/United – To be forgiven is to be set free from our sin debt. Jesus paid our sin debt in full at the cross. "If we confess our sins, He is faithful and just to forgive us our sins and cleanse us from all unrighteousness."[535] Having been forgiven we are free to be reconciled with God. To be reconciled means to be restored to peace, friendship, and harmony. On the cross Jesus suffered the penalty for your sin and my sin. Sinful man is an enemy, alienated from God, and dead in trespasses and sin. But on the cross Jesus suffered death, the wages of sin as our substitute. And when you by faith repent and ask the Lord for mercy to be your Savior and Lord, He will forgive you and reconcile you with God. You are then united and entwined with Jesus in a living/organic relationship. "For you were bought at a price; therefore, glorify God in your body and your spirit, which are God's.[536] "If anyone is in Christ, he is a new creature; all things are passed away; and behold all things are made new."[537]

4. Regenerated/Sealed – Once a person repents and asks Jesus to be his or her Savior and Lord, God declares that person righteous, that is, he or she is justified and accounted righteous. That person is forgiven for their sin and reconciled with God, and united in the covenantal relationship with the Lord Jesus Christ. Being reconciled with God and united in a covenantal relationship is the foundation upon which regeneration is made possible. At this juncture ask for

---

533. Psa. 103:12; 2 Cor. 5:21.
534. Rom. 4:5.
535. 1 John 1:9.
536. 1 Cor. 6:20.
537. 2 Cor. 5:17.

the gift of the Holy Spirit to come and live in your heart. The indwelling of the Holy Spirit regenerates the life of God within you and His presence is God's guarantee that seals your eternal future as a child of God.[538]

5. Power/Authority – The wisdom of the cross made the legal provisions to restore the God-given dominion that Adam forfeited when he disobeyed God. Jesus Christ has been given all authority in heaven and on earth.[539] Jesus "disarmed principalities and powers, he made a public spectacle of them, triumphing over them in it."[540] In other words, the devil's authority over mankind ended at the cross. Jesus instructed His disciples to tarry in Jerusalem until they were endued with power from on high.[541] The power that Jesus was referring to was the presence and power of the Holy Spirit. That same Spirit that had anointed Him for ministry following His water baptism would be poured upon believers when the Day of Pentecost had fully come.[542] "And these signs will follow those who believe. In My Name they will cast out demons; they will speak with new tongues, they will take up serpents, and if they drink any deadly thing, it will by no means hurt them; they will lay hands on the sick, and they will recover."[543] "And with great power the apostles gave witness to the resurrection of the Lord Jesus. And great grace was upon them all."[544]

The focus of this chapter has been "Steps of Faith". The emphasis is upon the responsibility of believers in Jesus Christ to participate with God through steps of faith rather than being passive. God in

538. Eph. 1:14; 2 Cor. 5:5.
539. Matt. 28:18.
540. Col. 2:15.
541. Luke 24:49.
542. Acts 1:5-8.
543. Mark 16:17-18.
544. Acts 4:33.

His wisdom sent His Son to be an atonement/propitiation for our sin through His death burial, resurrection, and ascension. "Steps of Faith" are the means by which God accepts sinners like you and me to participate in what Jesus accomplished in our behalf. Our salvation is dependent upon taking the above "Steps of Faith". The next chapter will address the "Places of Rest".

CHAPTER 6

The Cross and Places of Rest

"There remains therefore a rest for the people of God. For he who has entered His rest has himself also ceased from his works as God *did* from His. Let us therefore be diligent to enter that rest, lest anyone fall according to the same example of disobedience." (Hebrews 4:9-11)

"Oh, the depth of the riches both of the wisdom and knowledge of God! How unsearchable *are* His judgments and His ways past finding out!" (Romans 11:33)

HAVING DISCUSSED GOD'S "ACTS of Grace" and man's required "Steps of Faith," to participate in those acts of grace, we turn our attention to the third category of the atonement, "Places of Rest." These places of rest are not entered into by the cessation of work but through faith. The Children of Israel heard the gospel, but it did not profit them because they failed to mix what they heard with faith.[545]

---

545. Heb. 4:1-2.

Part Three: *Places of Rest*

The believer's "Places of Rest" are in Jesus Christ our Lord. The focus of this "rest" is not a one-day-a-week rest or an end-of-the-age rest, but on the Lord's provisions for daily rest through the atoning work of Jesus Christ. Because of what Jesus accomplished through His death, burial, and resurrection we are no longer slaves to sin, but liberated from that bondage and commanded to be diligent to enter the rest Jesus has provided. It is a tactic of the enemy to fill our daily lives with activities that drain our energies, challenge us with issues intended to weaken our faith, and instigate confusion into our circumstances that promote anxieties, fears, and anger, to the point of blaming God for our problems. Blaming God equates with unbelief, and unbelief is the source of unrest.

Never forget there is a daily rest in Christ and a future rest at the end of the age after the devil is cast into hell. Meanwhile, George Eldon Ladd states a fundamental principle of the kingdom of God: "God's reign manifests itself both in the future and in the present and thereby creates both a future realm and a present realm in which men may experience the blessings of His reign."[546] In other words there is both a "now" and "not yet" aspect to the kingdom of God. The issue being addressed in this chapter is the "now" aspect of the rest that we have in Jesus Christ.

We are experiencing that period of history in which Jesus prophesied that "men's hearts failing them from fear and the expectation of those things which are coming on the earth, for the powers of

---

546. George Eldon Ladd, *The Gospel of the Kingdom: Scriptural Studies in the Kingdom of God* (Grand Rapids, MI: William B. Eerdmans Publishing Company, 1977), 24.

heaven will be shaken."[547] The Lord's "shaking the powers of heaven" according to Richard C. Blight, "describes the historical overthrow of earthly nations and empires."[548] As our government and all other governments of the world are being shaken by the Lord in preparation for the second coming of Jesus. We will experience unexpected wars, pandemics, economic troubles, and lawlessness. But for those who put their trust in the Lord Jesus Christ, God has provided a place of rest even during the shaking of world governments. "The LORD also will roar from Zion and utter His voice from Jerusalem; The heavens and earth will shake; but the LORD will be a shelter for His people, and the strength of the children of Israel."[549] Jesus said, "Take My yoke upon you and learn from Me, for I am gentle and lowly in heart, and you will find rest for your souls."[550]

Covenant:

Through faith in Jesus, our resurrected Lord, a rest is available each day, but believer's must be diligent and intentional to enter His rest. One cannot be passive and expect to enter the Lord's daily rest. "Take My yoke upon you" is an aorist active imperative. That is an imperative that Jesus commanded in the past and remains in effect through the present. The question is, "What is this yoke about which Jesus commands?" "A yoke is an emblem of servitude; to couple any two things together in service."[551] Jesus Himself came "to serve and

---

547. Luke 21:26.

548. Richard C. Blight, *An Exegetical Summary of Luke 12–24*, 2nd ed. (Dallas, TX: SIL International, 2008), 388.

549. Joel 3:16; Isa. 4:6; Psa. 61:3; Psa. 143:9.

550. Matt. 11:29.

551. Zodhiates, *The Complete Word Study*.

give His life a ransom for many."[552] Jesus also said, "If anyone desires to be first, he shall be last of all and servant of all."[553] Jesus isn't simply looking for servants but servants who willingly commit themselves to the will of the Father, just as He expressed His commitment with the words "Not My will, but Yours be done."[554] That depth of commitment requires a covenantal relationship as in a marriage. The Apostle Paul states, "Do not be yoked together with unbelievers."[555] The context in which both Jesus and Paul use the term, "yoke" refers to a covenantal bond. Jesus further strengthens the necessity of being yoked in a covenantal relationship with Him by stating:

> "Most assuredly, I say to you, unless you eat the flesh of the Son of Man and drink His blood, you have no life in you. Whoever eats My flesh and drinks My blood has eternal life, and I will raise him up at the last day. For My flesh is food indeed, and My blood is drink indeed. He who eats My flesh and drinks My blood abides in Me, and I in him. As the living Father sent Me, and I live because of the Father, so he who feeds on Me will live because of Me. This is the bread which came down from heaven--not as your fathers ate the manna and are dead. He who eats this bread will live forever." (John 6:53-58).

Kenneth O. Gangel states, "We might paraphrase Jesus' words as, 'The one who keeps on feeding on Me will live because I live within

---

552. Mark 10:45.
553. Mark 9:35.
554. Luke 22:42.
555. 2 Cor. 6:14.

him.'"[556] F. F. Bruce states, "Jesus here defines what is meant by eating His flesh and drinking His blood. This language denotes that faith-union by which a mutual indwelling... of Jesus and His people is established."[557] Bruce's words "faith-union" and "mutual indwelling" agree with what Jesus describes as "abiding in Him" and "taking His yoke." Jesus' words and Bruce's interpretation of Jesus' words, both imply a covenant relationship. This covenant relationship is further emphasized by Jesus at the last supper.

> "And as they were eating, Jesus took bread, blessed and broke it, and gave it to the disciples and said, 'Take, eat; this is My body.' Then He took the cup, and gave thanks, and gave it to them, saying, 'Drink from it, all of you. For this is My blood of the new covenant, which is shed for many for the remission of sins.'" (Matthew 26:26-28).

In other words, the new covenant is established through the broken body and shed blood of Jesus. And the new covenant is the "yoke" that Jesus invites you and me to take upon us. It is from within the boundaries of the new covenant we find our place of daily rest. "I have been crucified with Christ; it is no longer I who live, but Christ lives in me; and the *life* which I now live in the flesh I live by faith in the Son of God, who loved me and gave Himself for me."[558] Rest is not the cessation of work, but faith in the finished work of Jesus

---

556. Kenneth O. Gangel, *John*, vol. 4, Holman New Testament Commentary (Nashville, TN: Broadman & Holman Publishers, 2000), 130.

557. F. F. Bruce, *The Gospel of John & Epistles of John* (Grand Rapids, MI: William B. Eerdmans Publishing Company, 2001), 160.

558. Gal. 2:20.

Christ that energizes and sustains our strength and well-being, even in the midst of gathering the harvest and overcoming the enemies of our soul. Jesus said, "My food is to do the will of Him who sent Me and finish His work."[559] The Apostle Paul understood this principle. Through his service to the Lord, he suffered many attacks and all kinds of persecution.[560] But, his conclusion was, "Most gladly I will rather boast in my infirmities, that the power of Christ may rest upon me."[561]

The new covenant is more than a doctrine, it is a personal relational bond with our heavenly Father, initiated by His love and continues by sustaining the strength and vitality of all who trust the Lord regardless of circumstances. We are not saved to simply get to heaven, as important as that is. We are saved to produce fruit by serving God and each other.[562] "For as the body without the spirit is dead, so faith without works is dead also."[563] However, we are not called to "do our own thing," but to deny ourselves, take up our cross daily, and follow Jesus.[564] We do not lead Jesus, He leads us and is the example for us. Jesus Himself said, "the Son can do nothing of Himself, but what He sees the Father do; for whatever He does, the Son also does in like manner."[565] We are not called to be lone rangers nor self-appointed superintendents of the kingdom. Jesus said,

> "Not everyone who says to Me, 'Lord, Lord,' shall enter the kingdom of heaven, but he who does the

---

559. John 4:34.
560. 2 Cor. 11:23-30.
561. 2 Cor. 12:9.
562. John 15:8.
563. James 2:26.
564. Matt. 16:24.
565. John 5:19.

will of My Father in heaven. Many will say to Me in that day, 'Lord, Lord, have we not prophesied in Your name, cast out demons in Your name, and done many wonders in Your name?' And then I will declare to them, 'I never knew you; depart from Me, you who practice lawlessness!'" (Matthew 7:21-23)

We are to be yoked together with Jesus just as a husband and wife are yoked together in the covenant of marriage. Notice how the early church accomplished so much. "And they went out and preached everywhere, the Lord working with *them* and confirming the word through the accompanying signs."[566] In other words the early disciples were yoked with Jesus in the ministry of the proclamation of the gospel. Jesus commands us to take His yoke upon our necks and learn of Him.[567] Co-laboring with Jesus means trusting and resting in His capacity to fulfill His will through you and me, not struggling to fulfill our personal agenda. "Therefore, since a promise remains of entering His rest, let us fear lest any of you seem to have come short of it."[568]

Being yoked together with the Lord Jesus and serving His agenda is the doorway into the rest provided by the new covenant. Jesus said, "And whoever gives one of these little ones only a cup of cold *water* in the name of a disciple, assuredly, I say to you, he shall by no means lose his reward."[569] The Apostle Paul understood being "yoked" together with the Lord Jesus in the New Covenant. When others tried

---

566. Mark 16:20.
567. Matt 11:29.
568. Heb. 4:1.
569. Matt. 10:42.

to persuade him not to go to Jerusalem at the conclusion of his third missionary journey, he responded by saying,

> And see, now I go bound in the spirit to Jerusalem, not knowing the things that will happen to me there, except that the Holy Spirit testifies in every city, saying that chains and tribulations await me. But none of these things move me; nor do I count my life dear to myself, so that I may finish my race with joy, and the ministry which I received from the Lord Jesus, to testify to the gospel of the grace of God. (Acts 20:22-24)

The Apostle was steadfast in his commitment to co-labor with the Lord in fulfilling the ministry/service which he had received from the Lord. And years later when Paul knew that he was about to be executed, he said, "I have fought the good fight, I have finished the race, I have kept the faith. Finally, there is laid up for me the crown of righteousness, which the Lord, the righteous Judge, will give to me on that Day...."[570] Andrew Murray urges believers to "Be earnest, put your whole heart into it, see that you do it; enter into rest."[571] It is through faith in Jesus Christ that you abide in covenantal rest that proceeds from the reality that "you died, and your life is hidden with Christ in God." You are seated with Jesus at the right hand of God "far above all principality and power and might and dominion, and every name that is named, not only in this age but also in that which is to come."[572] "For he who has entered His rest has himself also ceased

---

570. 2 Tim. 4:7-8.
571. Murray, *The Holiest of All*, 155.
572. Eph. 1:21, 2:6.

from his works as God *did* from His."[573] The Apostle Paul did not say "I can do all things by myself." No! He said, "I can do all things through Christ who strengthens me."[574] While we remain on this earth, co-laboring or yoked with the Lord Jesus in the New Covenant, we are to enjoy rest, for His yoke is easy and His burden is light.[575]

Peace/Joy:

Now, we will look at the peace of God and the joy of the Lord as places of rest provided by the Lord. God Himself is the fountain of peace and the sum of all excellence. After the Angel of the Lord miraculously revealed Himself to Gideon at Ophrah, Gideon built an altar to the Lord, and called it "The-Lord-Is-Peace" or "Jehovah-Shalom."[576] Nathan Stone states, "This word "Shalom" is most often and most appropriately translated "peace" some 170 times. It expresses the deepest desire of the human heart. It represented the greatest measure of contentment and satisfaction in life."[577] Later Isaiah gave a Messianic prophecy revealing that one of the names of the Messiah would be "Prince of Peace."[578] And the New Testament reveals that "the kingdom of God is not eating and drinking, but righteousness, peace and joy in the Holy Spirit."[579]

Since the disobedience of Adam, sin not only separated humanity from God, but all human hearts became hostile toward God to the extent "there is none who seeks after God. They have all turned

---

573. Heb. 4:10.
574. Phil. 4:13.
575. Matt. 11:38.
576. Judges 6:22-24.
577. Nathan Stone, *Names of God* (Chicago, IL: Moody Press, 1944), 113.
578. Isa. 9:6.
579. Rom. 14:17.

aside; They have together become unprofitable; There is none who does good, no, not one."[580] Even though mankind sometimes proclaims peace, the reality is "'There is no peace' says my God, 'for the wicked.'"[581] "Destruction and misery are in their ways; and the way of peace they have not known."[582] "Therefore justice is far from us, nor does righteousness overtake us; We look for light, but there is darkness! For brightness, *but* we walk in blackness!"[583] The point is that outside of a personal relationship with God through the atonement made by Jesus at the cross there is only a false peace. The contentment and satisfaction, about which Nathan Stone speaks above, is not known at all by anyone outside of the New Covenant. The concept of peace, both within the Old Testament word "*Shalom*" and the New Testament word "*Eirene*," approximates closely with the idea of salvation.[584]

May we never lose sight of the reality that "God is love,"[585] and neither sin nor mankind's hostility towards Him has ever diminished who He is. Therefore, amid this sinful world and man's hostility towards God, He continues to love every person. And in the fullness of time the "arm of the Lord" was made manifest, and a Savior was born as the heavenly host praised God saying, "Glory to God in the highest, And on earth peace, goodwill toward men!"[586] Thus, peace is "a conception distinctly peculiar to Christianity, the tranquil state of a

---

580. Rom. 3:11-12.

581. Isa. 48:22, 57:21.

582. Rom. 3:16-17.

583. Isa. 59:9.

584. See: Colin Brown, *The International Dictionary of New Testament Theology*, vol. 2, (Grand Rapids, MI: Zondervan, 1986) 777.

585. 1 John 4:7-8.

586. Luke 2:14.

soul assured of its salvation through Christ, and so fearing nothing from God and content with its earthly lot, of whatever sort that is."[587]

"All we like sheep had gone astray; We had turned, everyone, to his own way; And the LORD laid on Him the iniquity of us all."[588] God could not answer Jesus' prayer for the removal of the "cup"[589] of suffering, because it was impossible for our holy God to simply ignore sin. Sin had to be eradicated for peace to be restored. Jesus closed the breach caused by sin between God and mankind through His blood shed on the cross.[590] At the cross God's holy wrath was satisfied to the extent that for all who put their trust in Jesus Christ are no longer considered enemies of God, but now friends of God.[591] In other words, at the cross God resolved the offense that sin perpetrated against Him by condemning sin in the flesh,[592] and pouring out of His judgment upon Jesus, who willingly suffered that judgment as our substitute. "He *was* wounded for our transgressions, *He was* bruised for our iniquities; The chastisement for our peace *was* upon Him, And by His stripes we are healed."[593]

"Therefore, having been justified by faith, we have peace with God through our Lord Jesus Christ, through whom also we have access by faith into this grace in which we stand, and rejoice in hope of the glory of God."[594] Being justified by faith through the atoning work of Jesus brings the believer into an eternal state of grace which

---

587. Walter A. Elwell, *Evangelical Dictionary of Theology: Second Edition* (Grand Rapids, MI: Baker Academic, 2001), 897.
588. Isa. 53:6, paraphrased.
589. Matt. 26:38-42; Mark 14:35-36; Luke 22:39-42.
590. Col. 1:20.
591. John 15:15.
592. Rom. 8:3.
593. Isa. 53:5.
594. Rom. 5:1-2.

includes peace and the hope of glory. We are justified by faith and faith is a present grasp of a future reality. Hope is always future, and the "hope of glory" is the source of joy and rejoicing even in the face of painful trials and tribulations. Just as Jesus endured the cross, despising the shame "for the joy that was set before Him."[595] So, you are seeing how the peace that Jesus secured through His sacrifice on the cross positions' believers in a relationship with God that is peaceable and without hostility, but not yet complete. The best is yet to come! The anticipation of the hope of glory releases the joy of the Lord in our hearts which in turn strengthens us to endure the conflicts of the present.[596] Deliverance from the bondage of sin that alienates us from God our Creator and obtaining the security of peace with God are the headwaters for joy and rejoicing!

At the last supper Jesus said, "Peace I leave with you, My peace I give to you; not as the world gives do I give to you. Let not your heart be troubled, neither let it be afraid."[597] R. C. Lenski states, "The security and the well-being intended by this peace relates to far more than to protection in the hour of danger; it refers to the relation of the disciples to God."[598] This peace is one of the grand perfections of God's nature and the fortress where believers find rest. We are in agreement with the Psalmist in saying, "The LORD is my shepherd; I shall not want. He makes me to lie down in green pastures; He leads me beside the still waters."[599] Isaiah prophesied that God "will keep *him* in perfect peace, *whose* mind *is* stayed *on You*, because he trusts

595. Heb. 12:1-2.
596. Neh. 8:10.
597. John 14:27.
598. R. C. H. Lenski, *The Interpretation of St. John's Gospel* (Minneapolis, MN: Augsburg Publishing House, 1961), 1017.
599. Psa. 23:1-2.

in You.... For the Lord is everlasting strength."[600] Therefore, "Be anxious for nothing, but in everything by prayer and supplication, with thanksgiving, let your requests be made known to God; and the peace of God, which surpasses all understanding, will guard your hearts and minds through Christ Jesus."[601]

Access/Vision:

The wonderful thing that transpired while the children of Israel were at the foot of Mount Sinai and Moses was before the Lord on the top of the mountain, was that God not only gave Moses the Ten Commandments, but also gave him the pattern for the construction of the Tabernacle, so He could for the first time since the Garden of Eden dwell among men.[602] There was one important limitation, and that was only the High Priest was permitted to enter the Holy of Holies and only one day a year, on the Day of Atonement. And God said, "There I will meet with you, and I will speak with you from above the mercy seat, from between the two cherubim which *are* on the ark of the Testimony...."[603] The ark of the testimony was situated behind the veil in the holy of holies. The point is that God did dwell among the children of Israel, but they only had limited access to His presence. God through the ages had visited with men like Enoch, Noah, and Abraham, but had not dwelt among men since Adam's exposition from the Garden of Eden. How blessed Israel was among the nations of the world that God would dwell among them and meet with their high priest on the Day of Atonement. On the Day of Atonement their

600. Isa. 26:3-4.
601. Phil. 4:6-7.
602. Exod. 25:8, 29:46.
603. Exod. 25:22.

sins were forgiven, but the high priest had to carry out that same ritual year after year.

However, when Jesus laid His life down and shed His precious blood on the cross, everything changed. Jesus our High Priest, after the order of Melchizedek, serves according to the power of an endless life. Jesus did not serve in the Tabernacle on earth but presented Himself before the throne of God in heaven, not with the blood of goats and calves, but with His own sinless blood, and "this He did once and for all," "having obtained eternal redemption."[604] Andrew Murray states regarding the rituals on the Day of Atonement, and "in contrast with the daily ever-repeated sacrifices, Jesus accomplished all when He offered Himself once. That which has to be repeated is imperfect; that which need be done only once is perfect and lasts forever."[605] Raymond Brown sums up what Jesus has accomplished and continues to accomplish for us with the following comments.

> Jesus, the 'pioneer' of our salvation brings us to eternal glory by a saving route; we have been saved, we are being saved, and we shall be saved. Our present salvation is in Christ, but we must appropriate this blessing and *be what we are*. The author of Hebrews insists that Christ can save his readers from sin, fear, disobedience, apostasy, and apathy. He is the source of their present salvation. He rescues us, not only in the moment of initial commitment, but day by day and moment by moment. We must constantly renew

---

604. Heb. 7:27, 9:12.
605. Murray, *The Holiest of All*, 256.

our trust in Him, knowing that He will never fail us.[606]

As a result of Jesus pouring out His sinless blood on the cross, the veil in the earthly temple was rent from top to bottom. Jesus made a complete atonement (*propitiation and expiation*) for our sins once and for all. Kevin J. Conner states, "The rent veil speaks to us of the fact that the Way into the Holiest of All is now open to men.... The veil no longer stands as a separation between God and man. The middle wall of partition has been removed once and for all."[607] As a result, you and I are invited to "come boldly to the throne of grace, that we may obtain mercy and find grace to help in our time of need."[608] What an amazing invitation to confidently approach the throne of Almighty God, where grace and mercy are dispensed without the need for an angel or earthly priest to mediate for us.

Because of what Jesus accomplished for each of us at the cross we are invited to access the throne of Almighty God all day, every day, until the end of our days on this earth, and then we will join with all the others around God's throne to thank and worship Him forever! What marvelous access Jesus has opened for you and me into the glorious presence of our Father! Accessing His presence our vision is restored to see Him who is invisible and make our prayers and petitions. "Now this is the confidence that we have in Him, that if we ask anything according to His will, He hears us. And if we know that He hears us, whatever we ask, we know that we have the petitions that

---

606. Raymond Brown, *The Message of Hebrews*, John R. W. Stott, ed. (Downer Grove, IL: Inter-Varsity Press, 1982), 139.

607. Kevin J. Conner, *The Tabernacle of Moses* (Portland, OR: City Bible Publishing, 1976), 69.

608. Heb. 4:16.

we have asked of Him."[609] As believers, we are to make our request known to our heavenly Father with the assurance that He will charge His angels, the "ministering spirits sent forth to minister for those who will inherit salvation,"[610] to facilitate the answers to our prayers. Our confidence is even strengthened more, realizing that our heavenly Father "is able to do exceedingly abundantly above all that we ask or think...."[611] There, before the throne you cast all your cares upon Him, because He cares for you.[612] Access into God's presence is a privileged place for the release from the burdens of life and a secure place of rest for our soul. "He cares for you affectionately *and* cares about you watchfully,"[613] and no one is able to snatch you out of His hand.[614] Therefore, "Be anxious for nothing, but in everything by prayer and supplication, with thanksgiving, let your requests be made known to God; and the peace of God, which surpasses all understanding, will guard your hearts and minds through Christ Jesus."[615] When you access the presence of God and cast your cares upon Him, you will have entered a place of rest for your soul.

Adoption:

Every person is born into this world alienated from God because of our sin nature received from our parents, which they received from their parents, which goes all the way back to Adam and Eve. They were created with a pure and sinless nature, but their nature

---

609. 1 John 5:14-15.
610. Heb. 1:14.
611. Eph. 3:20.
612. 1 Peter 5:7.
613. *The Amplified Bible* (La Habra, CA: The Lockman Foundation, 1987), 1 Pe 5:7b.
614. John 10:29.
615. Phil. 4:6-7.

changed from pure and sinless to sinful and corrupt because of their disobedience in eating the forbidden fruit. But God, in His mercy had prepared before the foundation of the world a pathway of salvation for sinners. When by God's grace and through faith a person receives Jesus Christ as his or her Savior, and the Holy Spirit comes to live in his or her heart, that person is born again or regenerated being reconciled with God. But regeneration is distinguished from adoption in at least two ways. First, regeneration is to experience a new nature, whereby "old things have passed away; behold, all things have become new."[616] For the discussion on regeneration see Chapter Five. It is in regeneration that we receive the nature of a son of God. Second, adoption includes placement within the royal family of God. That is, placed in a position of responsibility within the family business.

> But when the fullness of the time had come, God sent forth His Son, born of a woman, born under the law, to redeem those who were under the law, that we might receive the adoption as sons. And because you are sons, God has sent forth the Spirit of His Son into your hearts, crying out, "Abba, Father!" (Galatians 4:4-6)

In our present-day culture, we think of adoption as bringing a child from outside of our family into our family structure. But Norman Geisler states that "*adoption* (Gal. 4:5) refers to the act of God that places a person as a son in God's family."[617] R. A. Torrey states,

---

616. 2 Cor. 5:17.
617. Geisler, *Systematic Theology, Volume Three*, 226.

"Etymologically the word translated "adoption" means "the placing a son.""[618] In other words we are born into the family of God as spiritual infants, and we receive the "Spirit of adoption." "For you did not receive the spirit of bondage again to fear, but you received the Spirit of adoption by whom we cry out, 'Abba, Father.'"[619] Our born-again experience is a birthing into the family of God. Our responsibility as a member of God's royal family is to "grow up" and mature "to the measure of the stature of the fullness of Christ; that we should no longer be children, tossed to and fro and carried about with every wind of doctrine, by the trickery of men, in the cunning craftiness of deceitful plotting."[620]

> For the earnest expectation of the creation eagerly **waits** for the revealing of the sons of God. For the creation was subjected to futility, not willingly, but because of Him who subjected *it* in hope; because the creation itself also will be delivered from the bondage of corruption into the glorious liberty of the children of God. For we know that the whole creation groans and labors with birth pangs together until now. Not only *that,* but we also who have the firstfruits of the Spirit, even we ourselves groan within ourselves, eagerly **waiting** for the adoption, the redemption of our body. (Romans 8:19-23; emphasis mine).

618. R. A. Torrey, *What the Bible Teaches a Thorough and Comprehensive Study of What the Bible Has to Say Concerning the Great Doctrines of Which It Treats* (New York, Chicago: Fleming H. Revell Company, 1898), 336.

619. Rom. 8:15.

620. Eph. 4:13-16.

As you can see that according to the above Scripture that "creation eagerly waits" and "we ourselves groan within ourselves, eagerly waiting for the adoption." In other words, all born-again believers received the "Spirit of adoption," when we were born-again. But we are waiting to be "placed" in the structure of the royal family of God when our redemption is complete. Our spiritual growth in the here and now is the Lord preparing each of us to fit functionally into the eternal governing structure of His royal family.

Our placement in God's royal family structure will take place following our resurrection at the second coming of the Lord Jesus. Our placement will be similar to the placement of Jesus after His resurrection and ascension. During His earthly ministry Jesus ministered as "God's beloved Son."[621] But upon Jesus' ascension God said, "I have set My King on My holy Hill of Zion."[622] Then God declared the decree: "The LORD has said to Me, 'You *are* My Son, Today I have begotten You. Ask of Me, and I will give *You* The nations *for* Your inheritance, And the ends of the earth *for* Your possession."[623]

Having chosen you and me in Christ "before the foundation of the world" and having "predestined us to adoption as sons by Jesus Christ to Himself," it is on the grounds of who Jesus is and what He has done that we are made worthy and have "the guarantee of our inheritance."[624] We are not only sons, we are also heirs of God and joint heirs with Jesus Christ.[625] Being heirs of God and joint heirs with Jesus establishes a secure place of rest for all believers. If the economy fails and devastation comes—our place of rest as heirs is so

---

621. Matt. 3:17; Mark 1:11; Luke 3:22.
622. Psa. 2:6.
623. Psa. 2:7-8; Acts 13:33.
624. Eph. 1:4-5, 11-14.
625. Rom. 8:17.

trustworthy that we can endure suffering for Jesus' sake and say with the Apostle Paul, "For our light affliction, which is but for a moment, is working for us a far more exceeding *and* eternal weight of glory."[626]

Liberty:

Liberty is one of the great ideals of the human heart, and God has made provision for every person to enjoy freedom from the bondage and oppression. When Jesus initiated His earthly ministry at Nazareth following His wilderness testings, He began by reading the following Scripture:

> The Spirit of the Lord GOD *is* upon Me, Because the LORD has anointed Me To preach good tidings to the poor; He has sent Me to heal the brokenhearted, To proclaim liberty to the captives, And the opening of the prison to *those who are* bound; To proclaim the acceptable year of the LORD." (Isaiah 61:1-2a; Luke 4:18-19).

After Jesus read Isaiah's prophecy He said, "Today this Scripture is fulfilled in your hearing."[627] Notice these three phrases: (1) "proclaim liberty to the captives," (2) "the opening of the prison to those who are bound," and (3) "to proclaim the acceptable year of the Lord" or "to proclaim the year of Jubilee." All three of these phrases pertain to the liberation of captives and the release from the oppression of the devil. It was for purpose of liberating men and women from the restraints of sin and bondage to the powers of darkness that Jesus was anointed

---

626. 2 Cor. 4:17.
627. Luke 4:21.

by the Holy Spirit. Therefore, when we review the earthly ministry of Jesus, we discover that He released His anointing through the following means: (1) the proclamation of truth, (2) healing the infirmed, (3) casting out demons, and finally, (4) "gave Himself a ransom for all."[628]

Jesus proclaimed truth, because He is the incarnation of truth. He said, "I am the way, the truth and the life."[629] Because of the deceptive power of the sin nature, men "exchanged the truth of God for the lie and worshiped and served the creature rather than the Creator...."[630] Jesus said to those who believed Him, "'If you abide in My word, you are My disciples indeed. And you shall know the truth, and the truth shall make you free.'"[631] The freedom that Jesus offers is described by J. P. Moreland and William Lane Craig as a freedom that "serves as a necessary condition for moral and some say intellectual responsibility.... or free will."[632] Think about the bondage experienced by all sinners and described by the Apostle Paul as follows:

> For I know that in me (that is, in my flesh) nothing good dwells; for to will is present with me, but *how* to perform what is good I do not find. For the good that I will *to do*, I do not do; but the evil I will not *to do*, that I practice. Now if I do what I will not *to do*, it is no longer I who do it, but sin that dwells in me. I find then a law, that evil is present with me, the one who wills to do good. For I delight in the law of God according to the inward man. But I see another

---

628. Matt. 20:28; Mark 10:45; 1 Tim. 2:6.
629. John 14:6.
630. Rom. 1:25.
631. John 8:31-32.
632. Moreland and Craig, *Philosophical Foundations*, 268.

law in my members, warring against the law of my
mind, and bringing me into captivity to the law of
sin which is in my members. O wretched man that
I am! Who will deliver me from this body of death?
(Romans 7:18-24)

Paul describes a situation whereby he wanted to do good but
found himself doing what he did not want to do; thereby recognizing
and confessing "sin dwells in me," and crying out, "O wretched man
that I am! Who will deliver me from this body of death?" Then he
draws his conclusion by identifying his Deliverer by saying, "I thank
God--through Jesus Christ our Lord!"[633] In other words Paul concluded that he could not deliver himself from the bondage of his own
wretchedness, but truth led him to Jesus Christ "who gave Himself a
ransom for all." The reality is that the truth that delivers you and me
from our sinful wretchedness and brings us into rest is more than a
proposition, it is a person, the Lord Jesus Christ. "For the law of the
Spirit of life in Christ Jesus has made me free from the law of sin and
death."[634] "And where the Spirit of the Lord is, there is liberty."[635] Colin
Kruse states,

The continuous and progressive transformation by
which believers are changed from one degree of glory to another is the moral transformation which is
taking place in their lives so that they approximate

---

633. Rom. 7:25.
634. Rom. 8:2.
635. 2 Cor. 3:17.

more and more to the likeness of God expressed so perfectly in the life of Jesus Christ.[636]

According to the Old Testament the children of Israel were confined to slavery under the Egyptians. But after the first Passover they were miraculously delivered from their slavery, crossing through the Red Sea on dry land. Now in the desert headed towards Mount Sinai the Lord God fed them supernaturally with manna. But on the sixth day they were instructed to gather enough for their needs on that day and also for the seventh day.[637] Because the seventh day was designated by God even before the giving of the Ten Commandments as a "Sabbath rest, a holy Sabbath to the Lord."[638] Jesus clarifies the reality of rest for the New Testament believer even further by stating, "The Sabbath was made for man, and not man for the Sabbath. Therefore, the Son of Man is also Lord of the Sabbath."[639] In other words believing in the Lord Jesus Christ breaks the bondage of sin and releases all believers into the Sabbath rest provided by Jesus Christ. "For you, brethren, have been called to liberty; only do not *use* liberty as an opportunity for the flesh, but through love serve one another."[640]

Summary: God has demonstrated His love for mankind through acts of grace whereby He has made provision for each person's salvation. In light of what God's grace has provided mankind must take steps of faith to appropriate God's gracious provisions in his or her life. Having taken the required steps of faith each believer is then prepared to enter God's provisions for rest. In this chapter we have

636. Colin Kruse, *Tyndale New Testament Commentaries, 2 Corinthians* (Grand Rapids, MI: Willian B. Eerdmans, 1997), 101.

637. Exod. 16:21-31.

638. Exod. 16:23.

639. Mark 2:27-28.

640. Gal. 5:13.

identified seven specific places of rest. The order in which we have discussed the places of rest is not of great importance. What is important is that every believer learn to enter and abide in the resting places that God has so graciously provided.

Jesus said, "Take My yoke upon you and learn from Me, for I am gentle and lowly in heart, and you will find rest for your souls."[641] We defined Jesus's yoke as accepting His invitation to enter into the New Covenant with Him. There is no other name given among men whereby we might be saved and enjoy rest from the bondage of sin. Being yoked together with the Lord Jesus and serving His agenda is the doorway into the places of rest provided by the New Covenant. His yoke is easy, and His burden is light.[642]

The second and third places of rest are found in the peace of God that passes our understanding and the joy of the Lord. "Being justified by faith we have peace with God through our Lord Jesus Christ, through whom also we have access by faith into this grace in which we stand and rejoice in hope of the glory of God."[643] Jesus said, "Peace I leave with you, My peace I give to you; not as the world gives do I give to you. Let not your heart be troubled, neither let it be afraid."[644] The peace of God is the sentinel that guards our hearts and keeps us in the place of rest even through the storms of life. The word of the Lord is: "You will keep *him* in perfect peace, *Whose* mind *is* stayed *on You*, Because he trusts in You."[645] And when our circumstances seem turbulent and our situation looks almost impossible, we need to keep ourselves in the peace of God and affirm that the "the joy of the

---

641. Matt. 11:29.
642. Matt. 11:30.
643. Rom. 5:1-2.
644. John 14:27.
645. Isa. 26:3.

Lord is our strength."[646] The adversary of our soul will try to disrupt our peace, steal our joy, and drive us from our place of rest. But he is a defeated foe, and our life is hidden with Christ in God, who is Jehovah-Shalom!

The fourth place of rest is in the very presence of God Almighty. "Jesus Christ came *as* High Priest of the good things to come, with the greater and more perfect tabernacle not made with hands, that is, not of this creation. Not with the blood of goats and calves, but with His own blood He entered the Most Holy Place once for all, having obtained eternal redemption."[647] Therefore, we are invited to "come boldly to the throne of grace, that we may obtain mercy and find grace to help in time of need."[648] Under the Old Covenant only the High Priest had access to God's presence and only once a year on the Day of Atonement. But under the terms of the New Covenant every believer has access to the very presence of God all day, every day! We are actually seated together with Christ in heavenly places "far above all principality and power and might and dominion, and every name that is named, not only in this age but also in that which is to come."[649] Forever seated in the place of restful security and vision, no longer under the authority or oppressive bondage of sin and the powers of darkness.

Our fifth place of rest is found in having received the "Spirit of Adoption." "For you did not receive the spirit of bondage again to fear, but you received the Spirit of adoption by whom we cry out, "Abba, Father.""[650] Adoption has to do with our placement within the

646. Neh. 8:10.
647. Heb. 9:11-12.
648. Heb. 4:16.
649. Eph. 1:21 and 2:6.
650. Rom. 8:15.

royal family of God. That is our place of service and authority in the government of God or our inheritance as the sons of God. We enter the family of God through the new birth. But we receive the Spirit of Adoption as we wait for the redemption of our bodies.[651] The rest we enjoy is the confidence we possess by receiving the Spirit of Adoption, the guarantee of our inheritance which will be made complete at the resurrection of our glorified bodies.

The final place of rest discussed in this chapter is liberty. Jesus came to proclaim, "liberty to the captives."[652] "Now the Lord is the Spirit; and where the Spirit of the Lord *is*, there *is* liberty."[653] Sin binds a person in slavery under the powers of darkness, just as the children of Israel were slaves to the Egyptians until they were liberated at the Passover. Slaves have no rest because they are always at the beck and call of their slave master. But every believer in Jesus Christ has been delivered from the bondage of slavery and entered the place of rest in the Lord Jesus Christ, who is our "Passover." Through His sacrificial death on the cross and by the power of His resurrection Jesus has liberated you and me from the bondage of sin and death.[654] "Therefore if the Son makes you free, you shall be free indeed."[655] "Stand fast therefore in the liberty by which Christ has made us free, and do not be entangled again with a yoke of bondage."[656]

Having discussed the places of rest for every believer provided for through the redemptive ministry of Jesus Christ, we will turn our attention in the next chapter to the hope of glory.

---

651. Rom. 8:23.
652. Luke 4:18
653. 2 Cor. 3:17.
654. 1 Cor. 5:7.
655. John 8:36.
656. Gal. 5:1.

The Cross and the Hope of Glory

"If in this life only we have hope in Christ, we are of all men the most pitiable. But now Christ is risen from the dead, *and* has become the firstfruits of those who have fallen asleep. For since by man *came* death, by Man also *came* the resurrection of the dead. For as in Adam all die, even so in Christ all shall be made alive. But each one in his own order: Christ the firstfruits, afterward those *who are* Christ's at His coming." (1 Corinthians 15:19-23)

HAVING DISCUSSED GOD'S "ACTS of Grace," "Steps of Faith," and "Places of Rest," we now turn our attention to the forth category of the atonement, the "Hope of Glory." We have "all sinned and fallen short of the glory of God."[657] But because of what Jesus has accomplished through His death, burial, resurrection, and ascension we now "rejoice in the hope of the glory of God."[658]

---

657. Rom. 3:23.
658. Rom 5:2.

Part Four: *The Hope of Glory*

Hope is more than a mere wish. Hope is the confident expectation that what God has promised He will fulfill, and hope is always future.

> Blessed *be* the God and Father of our Lord Jesus Christ, who according to His abundant mercy has begotten us again to a **living hope** through the resurrection of Jesus Christ from the dead, to an inheritance incorruptible and undefiled and that does not fade away, reserved in heaven for you, who are kept by the power of God through faith for salvation ready to be revealed in the last time. (1 Peter 1:3-5; emphasis mine).

In other words, death does not have the final say, because death was swallowed up in victory by the resurrection of Jesus Christ. "But each one in his own order: Christ the firstfruits, afterward those *who are* Christ's at His coming."[659] Death no longer has dominion over believers in the Lord Jesus Christ. While Jesus tarries all believers will experience physical death. However, physical death for believers in Jesus Christ is not an end, but a transition out of the temporal realm into the eternal realm of glory. "We are confident, yes, well pleased rather to be absent from the body and to be present with the Lord."[660] When we believers die, our physical bodies will go to a grave, but our spirit and soul will immediately go to be with the Lord. There in heaven the Lord has a place prepared for each of us as we wait for the

659. 1 Cor. 15:23.
660. 2 Cor. 5:8.

resurrection and glorification of our body which will be incorruptible and immortal.[661] Biblical hope is the bridge that connects our present temporal existence with our future glory that will be revealed at the second coming of Jesus. And Jesus' second coming will probably occur at the Father's appointed Feast of Trumpets as the following Scripture describes:

> For the Lord Himself will descend from heaven with a shout, with the voice of an archangel, and with the trumpet of God. And the dead in Christ will rise first. Then we who are alive *and* remain shall be caught up together with them in the clouds to meet the Lord in the air. And thus we shall always be with the Lord. (1 Thessalonians 4:16-17)

As we wait in expectation for that glorious morning when the trumpet will sound an the dead in Christ shall arise, our bodies shall be changed in a moment and a twinkling of an eye. The hope of our resurrection and the glory we will experience serves as an anchor that secures our soul through the storms of life just as an anchor secures a ship during a storm at sea.[662] Jesus died on the cross, was buried in a tomb, but on the third day He arose from the dead and ascended into heaven. He is coming again to receive us as His bride.[663] Our hope is anchored in the fulfillment of the prophecy in Daniel, chapter nine that includes the following events; (1) To finish the transgression, (2) To make an end of sins, (3) To make reconciliation for iniquity, (4) To bring everlasting righteousness, (5) To seal up the vision and

---

661. 1 Cor. 15:51-57; John 14:1-3.
662. Heb. 6:19.
663. Rev. 21:9.

prophecy, and (6) To anoint the Most Holy (place).[664] Kevin Conner states, "Here in this kind of a kingdom, these things come to absolute fulness. All are made possible judicially at Calvary, but now all will be seen actually in the Millennial age."[665] Satan will be bound during this one thousand years and the curse of death broken as the earth is restored to a Garden of Eden quality. This is our glorious future and hope. "Beloved, now we are children of God; and it has not yet been revealed what we shall be, but we know that when He is revealed, we shall be like Him, for we shall see Him as He is. And everyone who has this hope in Him purifies himself, just as He is pure."[666]

Immortality:

Adam was created as a mortal man with a free will and given the privilege of choosing to obey God or disobey Him. "And the LORD God commanded the man, saying, 'Of every tree of the garden you may freely eat; but of the tree of the knowledge of good and evil you shall not eat, for in the day that you eat of it you shall surely die.'"[667] Adam disobeyed God by eating the forbidden fruit. "Therefore, just as through Adam's disobedience, sin entered the world, and death through sin, and thus death spread to all men, because in Adam all mankind inherited a sin nature and have sinned."[668] It was by the grace and wisdom of God that mankind was granted the privilege of dying and being resurrected from the dead. Mankind is a human being, unlike angels who are spirit beings. Spirit beings have no capacity

---

664. Dan. 9:24.

665. Kevin J. Conner, *The Christian Millennium: Studies in Eschatological Millennial Views* (K. J. C. Publications, 2000), 221.

666. 1 John 3:2-3.

667. Gen. 2:16-17.

668. Rom. 5:12, paraphrased.

for physical death, and thus no possibility of being redeemed or born again. Therefore, when an angel sins, that angel has no capacity to pay the wages of sin, because they cannot shed blood, and "without shedding of blood there is no remission" of sin.[669] Hence, when angels sin against God they have no hope of redemption and are doomed to eternal damnation. "For the wages of sin is death."[670]

Mankind's physical death is the result of sin that has infected every aspect of our flesh, but God has provided a plan of redemption for us. If Adam had not sinned but had eaten from the tree of life, he would still be living today. After Adam sinned, "the LORD God said, 'Behold, the man has become like one of Us, to know good and evil. And now, **lest he put out his hand and take also of the tree of life, and eat, and live forever.**"[671] (Emphasis mine). So, God drove out the man; and He placed cherubim at the east of the garden of Eden, and a flaming sword which turned every way, to guard the way to the tree of life."[672] And Adam began working by the sweat of his brow until his physical body was overtaken by death at nine hundred and thirty years of age.[673]

One of the most painful experiences we suffer is when a loved one suddenly dies. Death is no respecter of persons, and no one is exempt. Death comes to the young as well as the elderly. Death disrupts our hopes and dreams, breaking precious family bonds including our covenant of marriage. Death causes grief so painful that even "Jesus wept" at the tomb of His friend Lazarus.[674] Scripture describes death

---

669. Heb. 9:22b
670. Rom. 6:23a.
671. Gen. 3:22.
672. Gen. 3:24.
673. Gen. 5:5.
674. John 11:35.

as "the last enemy,"[675] but the good news is that death does not have the final word, our resurrected Savior does! By the shedding of His sinless blood on the cross, His bodily resurrection from the grave, and the sprinkling of His precious blood before God in heaven, Jesus "abolished death and brought life and immortality to light"[676] for everyone who puts their faith and trust in Him as their personal Savior and Lord. When the Lord Jesus returns the dead in Christ shall be raised and "this corruptible has put on incorruption, and this mortal has put on immortality, then shall be brought to pass the saying that is written: 'Death is swallowed up in victory.'"[677] The reality is that bodily resurrection and immortality were included in the "hidden wisdom which God ordained before the ages for our glory, which none of the rulers of this age knew; for had they known, they would not have crucified the Lord of glory."[678] Walter Elwell provides the following insight into the issue of Biblical immortality.

> Immortality, for the Christian, involves the resurrection and may be fully attained only after it. While it is said that believers who have died are present with the Lord when they are absent from the body (2 Cor. 5:8), they are nevertheless to be changed at Christ's appearing. Both those who have died and those who are alive upon earth will receive a body like the resurrection body of Jesus Christ (Phil. 3:21). Those who are the children of God will be like Christ (1 John 3:2),

---

675. 1 Cor. 15:26.
676. 2 Tim. 1:10.
677. 1 Cor. 15:54.
678. 1 Cor. 2:7-8.

perfected in righteousness (Phil. 1:6), and they will serve God continually.[679]

Eternal life is a life that never ends. That is true, but that does not exhaust the meaning of immortality. Immortality includes the reality that we will live in an eternal state or condition in which we will not be capable of sinning nor dying. We will live in an environment of light with no darkness nor night. We will have no capacity to degenerate or decompose. Gordon D. Fee states, "The long chain of decay and death inaugurated by the first Adam will finally be irrevocably broken by the last Adam.... No more can death tyrannize, because it has been 'swallowed up' by resurrection."[680] And death itself will one day be "cast into the lake of fire. This is the second death. And anyone not found written in the Book of Life was cast into the lake of fire."[681] What a horrible destiny for any person to experience in light of the truth that the Lord Jesus has made every possible provision for every person to have immortal life and eternal glory in union with Him in a world without end. "Beloved, now we are children of God; and it has not yet been revealed what we shall be, but we know that when He is revealed, we shall be like Him, for we shall see Him as He is."[682] "Now to the King eternal, immortal, invisible, to God who alone is wise, *be* honor and glory forever and ever. Amen."[683]

---

679. Elwell, *Evangelical Dictionary*, 598.

680. Gordon D. Fee, *The First Epistle to the Corinthians: The New International Commentary on the New Testament* (Grand Rapids, MI: William B. Eerdmans Publishing Co., 1987), 803.

681. Rev. 20:14-15.

682. 1 John 3:2.

683. 1 Tim. 1:17.

Inheritance:

God is a giver, and it is always the Father's desire to bless His children. "God so loved the world that He gave His only begotten Son." Therefore, one of the disciplines that we as followers of Jesus must learn and cultivate is our willingness to give. Jesus taught that two powerful principles: (1) "It is more blessed to give than receive."[684] And (2) "Everyone who has left houses or brothers or sisters or father or mother or wife or children or lands, for My name's sake, shall receive a hundredfold, and inherit eternal life."[685] These two principles help us understand that we are God's stewards in this world, not owners. "The earth *is* the LORD'S, and all its fullness, The world and those who dwell therein."[686] So, everything belongs to God, but He gives us many good things to enjoy during this earthly journey.[687] The point is that the best we may enjoy in the here and now cannot be compared to the eternal glory we will receive as an inheritance from our heavenly Father.[688]

Our culture often gives honor and accolades to those individuals who accumulate significant amounts of property and wealth. And there isn't anything immoral about accumulating wealth except Jesus teaches us that riches are "deceitful."[689] Wealth may purchase pleasure and earthly possessions. But believers in Christ refuse to be shaped by our surrounding culture,[690] because the Scriptures reveal

684. Acts 20:35.
685. Matt. 19:29.
686. Psa. 24:1.
687. 1 Tim. 6:17
688. Rom. 8:18.
689. Matt. 13:22.
690. Rom. 12:1-2.

a future glory worth waiting for—the best is yet to come![691] It doesn't matter how much wealth a person accumulates, when death comes all earthly possessions are relinquished.[692] The greatest value we will ever enjoy will consist of our eternal inheritance from our heavenly Father.[693]

There is an incalculable difference between a son and an orphan. The reality is that a son has an inheritance, but an orphan does not. "He who overcomes shall inherit all things, and I will be his God and he shall be My son."[694] As the children of God, we are indeed so very grateful for the grace of God that brings salvation in the here and now. But "if in this life only we have hope in Christ, we are of all men the most pitiable."[695] Beyond the brevity and trials of this life on earth our Lord has promised us "a hope and a future!"[696] "In this you greatly rejoice, though now for a little while, if need be, you have been grieved by various trials, that the genuineness of your faith, *being* much more precious than gold that perishes, though it is tested by fire, may be found to praise, honor, and glory at the revelation of Jesus Christ."[697]

Our inheritance is the kingdom of God with all its blessings and glory. "Then the King will say to those on His right hand, 'Come, you blessed of My Father, inherit the kingdom prepared for you from the foundation of the world.'"[698] "While enjoyment of the kingdom of God begins in this life, insofar as the kingdom is already present,

---

691. 1 Cor. 2:7-10.
692. Matt. 6:19-20; Luke 12:23.
693. Rev. 21:7.
694. Rev. 21:7.
695. 1 Cor. 15:19.
696. Jer. 29:11.
697. 1 Peter 1:6-7.
698. Matt. 25:34.

the full possession is future."[699] The Holy Spirit is the member of the Godhead who guarantees our inheritance as heirs of God. "The Spirit Himself bears witness with our spirit that we are children of God, and if children, then heirs--heirs of God and joint heirs with Christ, if indeed we suffer with *Him*, that we may also be glorified together."[700] The Holy Spirit is "the guarantee of our inheritance until the redemption of the purchased possession."[701] "He, the Holy Spirit, was sent to the church after Christ's own entry into His inheritance at His ascension."[702]

"Christ Himself as the Son is the true heir; He has inherited a name above every name and has been appointed heir of all things.[703] But by God's grace, all who become His through faith are counted joint heirs with Jesus."[704] What Jesus accomplished through His crucifixion, burial, resurrection, and ascension does much more than achieve the possibility of the forgiveness of sins, as extremely important as that is. But through the shedding of His blood and presenting it before the mercy seat in heaven, Jesus has made reconciliation with the Father possible for all who will believe on Him, and thereby making us heirs and joint-heirs with Himself a reality.[705] Jesus came to earth the first time as a suffering servant, but He will return the second time as the King of kings and LORD of Lords. Therefore, we are exhorted to be "of one mind, having compassion for one another;

---

699. Elwell, *Evangelical Dictionary*, 608.

700. Rom. 8:16-17.

701. Eph. 1:14.

702. R. E. Nixon, "Inheritance," ed. D. R. W. Wood et al., *New Bible Dictionary* (Leicester, England; Downers Grove, IL: InterVarsity Press, 1996), 506.

703. Phil. 2:9; Heb. 1:4.

704. Walter A. Elwell and Philip Wesley Comfort, *Tyndale Bible Dictionary*, Tyndale Reference Library (Wheaton, IL: Tyndale House Publishers, 2001), 635.

705. Heb. 9:11-14.

love as brothers, *be* tenderhearted, *be* courteous; not returning evil for evil or reviling for reviling, but on the contrary blessing, knowing that you were called to this, that you may inherit a blessing."[706] The blessing we will inherit will include the glory of life eternal reigning with Jesus Christ forever and ever as members of God's royal family.

Reigning with Christ:

There is at this present time a dimension of our relationship with the Lord Jesus whereby we reign in life. "For if by the one man's offense death reigned through the one, much more those who receive abundance of grace and of the gift of righteousness will reign in life through the One, Jesus Christ."[707] However, suffering is also a part of our present relationship with Jesus. "For to you it has been granted on behalf of Christ, not only to believe in Him, but also to suffer for His sake."[708] Much of our suffering is the result of opposition from our adversary the devil. Hence the Apostle Peter exhorts us to "Be sober, be vigilant; because your adversary the devil walks about like a roaring lion, seeking whom he may devour."[709]

But the really good news is that when Jesus returns to earth the serpent of old, who is the Devil and Satan, will be bound and sealed in the bottomless pit for one thousand years. This thousand-year reign of Christ over the earth is a period of rest and blessedness for mankind. During that period believers will live and reign with Christ on the earth.[710] The thousand-year reign of Jesus and His bride equates

---

706. 1 Peter 3:8-9.
707. Rom. 5:17.
708. Phil. 1:29.
709. 1 Peter 5:8.
710. Rev. 20:1-4.

to the seventh day during the week of creation when God rested from all His work which He had done.[711] "And the earth will be filled with the knowledge of the glory of the LORD, as the waters cover the sea."[712] However, this does not exhaust our hope of glory because at the end of the thousand years the devil and his cohorts will be "cast into the lake of fire and brimstone.... And they will be tormented day and night forever and ever."[713] At that juncture there will be a new heaven and a new earth wherein dwells righteousness.[714] And Christ and His bride will reign forever and ever! That future is an anchor for our soul and our hope of glory![715]

Consider the conditions on the earth after the Lord Jesus returns and "the kingdoms of this world have become *the kingdoms* of our Lord and of His Christ."[716] "He shall judge between the nations, and rebuke many people; They shall beat their swords into plowshares, And their spears into pruning hooks; Nation shall not lift up sword against nation, Neither shall they learn war anymore."[717] The most recent century with world wars and international conflicts has devastated families, communities, and countries. War even now continues in several places in the world, including the Ukraine with destruction, suffering, and many tears. It is almost hard to imagine a world without war. But, when Jesus the Prince of Peace reigns on the earth men will not learn war anymore! Can you imagine what life will be like without the enormous amounts of financial resource being expended in military budgets around the world? What will it be like

711. Gen. 2:1-3.
712. Hab. 2:14.
713. Rev. 20:10.
714. Rev. 21:1-8; 2 Peter 3:13.
715. Heb. 6:19; Col. 1:27.
716. Rev. 11:15.
717. Isa. 2:4; Micah 4:3.

with the millions of personnel now restricted to military service and the purposes of war, being released to produce goods and services for the prosperity of all people?

When the Lord Jesus reigns in peace over the earth with His bride, the earth will become so productive that Amos the prophet declared, "the plowman shall overtake the reaper."[718] That means that the crops will be so abundant that it will be time to plow before all the harvest can be fully gathered. In other words when the devil is imprisoned and there is no more war, productivity will skyrocket! There will be no famines nor food shortages, but an abundance of good food for everyone! Remember when Moses sent the twelve spies into the Canaan Land, and it took two of those men to carry a bunch of grapes.[719] That is the kind of fruitfulness we will experience when we rule and reign with the Lord Jesus during the millennium. And this is just the beginning of the hope of glory—there is more—much more!!

Isaiah was given insight into the millennial reign of Jesus and saw the beauty and worder of wolf and lamb dwelling together![720] He also saw the calf and young lion along with a cow and bear grazing together. The lion who is characteristically carnivorous was eating straw like an ox. He saw nursing children playing with vipers, and the enmity that had existed since curse was placed upon the serpent after Adam and Eve had eaten the forbidden fruit, no longer existed and no one was being harmed.[721] David Guzik states,

> In Genesis 9:2–3, the Lord gave Noah, and all mankind after him, the permission to eat meat. At the

---

718. Amos 9:13.
719. Nun. 13:23.
720. Isa. 11:6-9.
721. Gen. 3:15; Isa. 11:6-10.

same time, the Lord put the *dread* of man in animals, so they would not be effortless prey for humans. Now, in the reign of the Messiah, that is reversed. For this reason, many think that in the reign of the Messiah, the Millennium, humans will return to being vegetarians, as it seems they were before Genesis 9:2–3.[722]

As Jesus the Prince of Peace reigns over the earth even the animals will be at peace with each other. "They shall not hurt nor destroy in all My holy mountain, For the earth shall be full of the knowledge of the LORD as the waters cover the sea."[723] Notice that the conditions of peace throughout the kingdom are linked directly to the "knowledge of the Lord" throughout the earth. As stated earlier there is a great difference between the present conditions on the earth and the glory that will prevail during the millennium. The reality is that the devil and his demons will be imprisoned and cannot deceive the nations anymore until the very end of the millennium.[724] But Jesus, the King of kings and Lord of lords will reign, and we, His bride, will reign with Him throughout the millennium and beyond through all eternity in the new heavens and earth! At the present time we are learning to serve the Lord and each other with the heart of a king. But we look forward when we will reign as kings with the heart of a servant like the Lord Jesus.

---

722. David Guzik, *Isaiah*, David Guzik's Commentaries on the Bible (Santa Barbara, CA: David Guzik, 2000), Isa. 11:6–9.

723. Isa. 11:9.

724. Rev. 20:3.

The Glorious Light:

God is the "Father of lights, with whom there is no variation or shadow of turning."[725] In other words, God being the "Father of lights" means the He is the ultimate source of light. "This is the message which we have heard from Him and declare to you, that God is light and in Him is no darkness at all."[726] Remember that on the first day of the creation week God said, "let there be light and there was light."[727] But the sun was not made and put in place until the fourth day.[728] Thus, from the first verses of the Bible and throughout Scripture, darkness characterizes the absence of God's presence and/or judgment.[729] For example, one of the ten plagues upon Egypt was darkness, and it was so dark that the darkness could be felt, and the Egyptians could not see one another for three days.[730] Another example is when Jesus spoke of the unprofitable servant being cast into the outer darkness where there will be weeping and gnashing of teeth.[731] But thanks be to God, who "has delivered us from the power of darkness and conveyed *us* into the kingdom of the Son of His love, in whom we have redemption through His blood, the forgiveness of sins."[732] "In Him was **life** (*zoe – not physical life but eternal spiritual life*), and the **life** *(zoe)*[733] was the **light** (*phos – source of light*) of men. And the

725. James 1:17.
726. 1 John 1:5.
727. Gen. 1:6.
728. Gen. 1:14-19.
729. Gen. 1:2, 15:12; Matt. 8:12, 22:13, 25:30.
730. Exod. 10:21-23.
731. Matt. 25:30
732. Col. 1:13-14.
733. John 1:4 (*zoe - The same kind of life that God breathed into Adam's nostrils in Genesis. 1:7. Life flows from God the Father through God the Son to you and me. God is the absolute source and cause of all life and light. John 5:26, 11:25, 12:50. See John 6:57*).

light shines in the darkness, and the darkness did not **comprehend** (*katalambano – overcome or overtake*) it."[734] (Emphasis mine).

God is pure Being as revealed by His name, "I Am".[735] His manifest presence is of such a pure quality of light that when He appeared to Moses in the burning bush, the bush appeared to be on fire, but it was not consumed.[736] Just as there appeared divided tongues of fire upon those in the upper room on the Day of Pentecost when God the Holy Spirit was poured upon them, but they were not burned.[737] Jesus said, "I am the light of the world. He who follows Me shall not walk in darkness, but in the light of life."[738] John the Baptist came to bear witness to Light. "He was not that Light, but *was sent* to bear witness of that Light. That was the true Light which gives light to every man coming into the world."[739]

When Jesus began His Galilean ministry,[740] the Scripture says, *"The people who sat in darkness have seen a great light, and upon those who sat in the region and shadow of death Light has dawned."*[741] In other words, Jesus by His words and deeds revealed God the Father of lights. "No one has seen God at any time. The only begotten Son, who is in the bosom of the Father, He has declared *Him*.[742] The point being there is a relationship between light and revelation. So, when Jesus ministered, the darkness was overcome with light and the captives of the darkness were released by the power of "the revelation of the mystery

---

734. John 1:4-5. Emphasis mine.
735. Exod. 3:14.
736. Exod. 3:1-5.
737. Acts 2:1-3.
738. John 8:12, 9:5, 11:9.
739. John 1:8-9.
740. John 9:5.
741. Matt. 4:16.
742. John 1:18.

kept secret since the world began."[743] Jesus said, "He who believes in Me, believes not in Me but in Him who sent Me. And he who sees Me sees Him who sent Me. I have come *as* a light into the world, that whoever believes in Me should not abide in darkness."[744]

We who trust in Jesus as Savior are often so concerned about getting our personal needs met that we overlook the awesome glory and majesty of God. "*He who is* the blessed and only Potentate, the King of kings and Lord of lords, who alone has immortality, dwelling in unapproachable light, whom no man has seen or can see, to whom *be* honor and everlasting power. Amen."[745] Arthur W. Pink states, "Such a One is to be revered, worshipped, and adored. He is solitary in His majesty, unique in His excellency, peerless in His perfections.... He gives to all and is enriched by none."[746]

> You therefore, beloved, since you know *this* beforehand, beware lest you also fall from your own steadfastness, being led away with the error of the wicked; **but grow in the grace and knowledge of our Lord and Savior Jesus Christ**. To Him *be* the glory both now and forever. Amen. (2 Peter 3:17-18, emphasis mine).

The glorious light addresses the issue of "revelation" or the "capacity to see Him who is invisible."[747] The Greek word for "revelation" is "*apokálupsis*", this "word, includes not merely the thing shown and

---

743. Rom. 16:25.
744. John 12:44-46.
745. 1 Tim. 6:15b-16
746. Arthur W. Pink, *Gleanings in the Godhead* (Chicago, Il: Moody Press, 1975), 13.
747. Heb. 11:27; Col. 1:15.

seen but the interpretation, the unveiling of the same."[748] The Holy Spirit is the Spirit of wisdom and revelation that enlightens our hearts and minds with revelation that transcends human knowledge and illuminates our pathway.[749] We live in a culture that places great emphasis on "scientific knowledge" or "empirical knowledge". That is knowledge obtained through observation. If it cannot be seen or weighed or measured, then it does not qualify as "knowledge". Since God is Spirit and cannot be seen, weighed, nor measured, then according to science, He must not exist.[750] Therefore, the knowledge of God is not valued in much of our culture. This lack of the knowledge of God is not a recent or new type of darkness, because the Scripture says, "it is written: *Eye has not seen, nor ear heard, Nor have entered into the heart of man The things which God has prepared for those who love Him.*"[751] Man in his intellectual arrogance "suppresses the truth in unrighteousness.... Professing to be wise, they became fools."[752] But for all who believe in God and act in faith, trusting His promises, God has revealed Himself to them through His Spirit. "For the Spirit searches all, yes, the deep things of God."[753] "But even if our gospel is veiled, it is veiled to those who are perishing, whose minds the god of this age has blinded, who do not believe, lest the light of the gospel of the glory of Christ, who is the image of God, should shine on them."[754]

For those individuals who reject the love of God and refuse to live in the light of the gospel will not participate in the hope of glory. "And this is the condemnation, that the light has come into the world,

748. Zodhiates, *The Complete Word Study.*
749. Eph. 1:17-21.
750. John 1:18, 6:46; 1 John 4:12.
751. 1 Cor. 2:9; Isa. 64:4.
752. Rom. 1:18-23.
753. 1 Cor. 2:7-10.
754. 2 Cor. 4:3-4.

and men loved darkness rather than light, because their deeds were evil."[755] But for all who believe on the Lord Jesus Christ as Savior, the hope of glory is a personal reality that sustains our faith through the trials of life. However, we cannot be passive and expect to be over-comers in this world. We are exhorted to "Fight the good fight of faith, lay hold on eternal life...."[756] For some individuals the darkness of the world system all around us, plus the ongoing tactics of the dev-il are so oppressive that fear crushes their faith, and hope is lost to despair. But believers in Jesus Christ are not ignorant of the schemes of the devil, and understand that "the night is far spent, the day is at hand. Therefore, let us cast off the works of darkness, and let us put on the armor of light."[757] "If we walk in the light as He is in the light, we have fellowship with one another, and the blood of Jesus Christ His Son cleanses us from all sin."[758] We as believers are not to receive the grace of God in vain,[759] nor lose sight of the exhortation given by the Apostle Paul.

> For I am persuaded that neither death nor life, nor angels nor principalities nor powers, nor things present nor things to come, nor height nor depth, nor any other created thing, shall be able to separate us from the love of God which is in Christ Jesus our Lord. (Romans 8:38-39)

---

755. John 3:19.
756. 1 Tim. 6:12a.
757. Rom. 13:12.
758. 1 John 1:7.
759. 2 Cor. 6:1.

Contrary to allowing our faith to be crushed by darkness, we by the grace of God and the empowerment of the Holy Spirit are committed to walking in the light of life and refuse to cast away our confidence. We are developing endurance, so that after we have done the will of God, we may receive the promise. Because, the Lord has said, "If anyone draws back, My soul has no pleasure in him. But we are not of those who draw back to perdition, but of those who believe to the saving of the soul."[760] And "the path of the just *is* like the shining sun, That shines ever brighter unto the perfect day."[761] "For it is the God who commanded light to shine out of darkness, who has shone in our hearts to *give* the light of the knowledge of the glory of God in the face of Jesus Christ."[762]

New Jerusalem:

One of the most foundational patterns revealing the redemptive purposes of God is the significance of "sevens" in Scripture. For example, seven days in the week of creation, seven pieces of furniture in the Tabernacle, seven Feast of Israel, plus many more sevens. Scripture also speaks of "weeks" in terms of "a period of seven units of time (Da 9:24, 25,26, 27)."[763] So, there are weeks of days, weeks of months, weeks of years, and weeks of 1,000s of years. Kevin J. Conner explains this Biblical concept of weeks as follows:

> The Hebrew mind was saturated with the concept of the "weeks of the Lord." The whole context of Scrip-

---

760. Heb. 10:38-39.
761. Prov. 4:18.
762. 2 Cor. 4:6.
763. James Swanson, *Dictionary of Biblical Languages.*

ture shows indeed that God was shadowing forth the "Redemptive Week" in the patterns of the sevens given to the chosen nation of Israel.... The Lord commanded Israel to work the land for six years, but the seventh year was to be a year of rest, a Sabbath for the land.... Failure to keep the Sabbath years of Rest for the land brought about the Babylonian Captivity for 70 years. This Captivity became the 70 Sabbaths for the land (2 Chro. 36:21; Dan. 9:1-2). Again, we have a "week", the "Week of years"; work the land six years, and the seventh year rest. This surely points to the "seventh Millennium" when the earth shall keep her Sabbath Rest, with the curse lifted and Satan bound.[764]

The goal of God's redemptive purposes is holy and uninhibited fellowship with His family. That is why Jesus defined the first and great commandment to be, "You shall love the Lord your God with all your heart, with all your soul, and with all your mind."[765] The church is an assembly of people called out of this world system, who love God and each other, and are betrothed as a chaste virgin to Jesus Christ, living in fervent expectation of His second coming and the "marriage supper of the Lamb."[766] Following the marriage supper of the Lamb, Jesus and His bride shall return to earth and the "kingdoms of this world shall become the kingdoms of our Lord and of His Christ," and He shall rule the nations with a rod of iron.[767] "And He (Jesus) has on

---

764. Conner, *The Christian Millennium, 196-197.*
765. Matt. 22:36-37.
766. 2 Cor. 11:2; Rev. 19:9.
767. Rev. 11:15; 19:15.

His robe and on His thigh a name written: KING OF KINGS AND LORD OF LORDS."[768] (Emphasis mine). Following the establishment of Jesus' kingdom on the earth, we the redeemed bride will rule and reign with the Lord Jesus for a thousand years as we have discussed earlier.

Following our millennial reign of the Lord Jesus the redemptive week of seven thousand years will be complete and there will be a new heaven and earth and a "New Jerusalem."[769] "Then He who sat on the throne said, 'Behold, I make all things new.' And He said to me, 'Write, for these words are true and faithful.' And He said to me, 'It is done! I am the Alpha and the Omega, the Beginning and the End.'"[770]

> And he carried me away in the Spirit to a great and high mountain, and showed me **the great city, the holy Jerusalem, descending out of heaven from God, having the glory of God. Her light** was **like a most precious stone, like a jasper stone, clear as crystal.** Also she had a great and high wall with twelve gates, and twelve angels at the gates, and names written on them, which are *the names* of the twelve tribes of the children of Israel: three gates on the east, three gates on the north, three gates on the south, and three gates on the west. Now the wall of the city had twelve foundations, and on them were the names of the twelve apostles of the Lamb.... The twelve gates *were* twelve pearls: each individual gate was of one pearl. **And the street of the city** was **pure gold, like trans-**

768. Rev. 19:16.
769. Rev. 21:1-2.
770. Rev 21:5-6a.

parent glass. **But I saw no temple in it, for the Lord God Almighty and the Lamb are its temple. The city had no need of the sun or of the moon to shine in it, for the glory of God illuminated it. The Lamb is its light. And the nations of those who are saved shall walk in its light,** and the kings of the earth bring their glory and honor into it. Its gates shall not be shut at all by day (there shall be no night there). (Revelation 21:10-14, 21-25, emphasis mine).

The "New Jerusalem" descending out of heaven from God marks a new era following the Millennium, because the first heaven and first earth pass away.[771] God's "week of redemption" or the seven thousand from creation through the end of the millennium now completed, the new era begins. This new era will be characterized by unhindered face to face fellowship between God and His redeemed royal family. "Then the righteous will shine forth as the sun in the kingdom of their Father...."[772] The Apostle John writes, "There shall be no night there: They need no lamp nor light of the sun, for the Lord God gives them light. And they shall reign forever and ever."[773] The Prophet Isaiah also declares, "The sun shall no longer be your light by day, nor for brightness shall the moon give light to you; But the LORD will be to you an everlasting light, and your God your glory."[774]

Other distinguishing characteristics of life in the New Jerusalem include the complete absence of darkness, death, sorrow, pain, and tears. It will be a city of eternal peace, blessedness, and

---

771. Psa. 102:13-14; Isa. 65:17; 2 Peter 3:10; Rev. 21:2, 10-11.
772. Matt. 13:43.
773. Rev. 22:5.
774. Isa. 60:19.

righteousness.[775] The bliss of the New Jerusalem ought not to be thought of as simply an intensification of the pleasures of this life, because God is making all things new. However, the primary feature of the New Jerusalem is living within the glorious presence of the Lord Himself. Life in the New Jerusalem is the hope of glory that anchors our souls through the challenges and storms of this present life. It is also extremely important for believers in Jesus Christ to remember that this beautiful city and the hope of glory is only possible for you and me because of what Jesus accomplished through His death, burial, resurrection, and ascension.

Summary:

The hope of glory is the bridge that connects our present relationship with God to the future He has prepared for us. Our hope is built on the rock-solid foundation of the death, burial, resurrection, and ascension of our Lord Jesus Christ. Jesus will return and receive His Church, His bride.

> For the Lord Himself will descend from heaven with a shout, with the voice of an archangel, and with the trumpet of God. And the dead in Christ will rise first. Then we who are alive *and* remain shall be caught up together with them in the clouds to meet the Lord in the air. And thus, we shall always be with the Lord. (1 Thessalonians 4:16-17).

This is not a wish, but a promise made by the Lord Jesus Himself. At the last supper just prior to His crucifixion Jesus told His disciples,

775. 2 Peter 3:13.

"I go to prepare a place for you. And if I go and prepare a place for you, I will come again and receive you to Myself; that where I am, *there* you may be also."[776] Jesus continued by saying, "A little while longer and the world will see Me no more, but you will see Me. Because I live, you will live also."[777] Then forty days after His death, burial, and resurrection while on the Mount of Olives speaking about the kingdom of God, He was taken up in a cloud out of their sight.

> "And while they looked steadfastly toward heaven as He went up, behold, two men stood by them in white apparel, who also said, 'Men of Galilee, why do you stand gazing up into heaven? This *same* Jesus, who was taken up from you into heaven, will so come in like manner as you saw Him go into heaven.'" (Acts 1:10-11).

When Jesus returns the dead in Christ shall arise and we who are alive shall be caught up together to meet the Lord in the air. At the moment of our resurrection, we shall be changed. "This corruptible must put on incorruption, and this mortal *must* put on immortality. So when this corruptible has put on incorruption, and this mortal has put on immortality, then shall be brought to pass the saying that is written: '*Death is swallowed up in victory.*'"[778] Immortality means that we will never again be subject to death, nor be capable of sinning or dying. But we will live and reign with Jesus forever.

The very best we have in this life is not to be compared with the glory we will receive as an inheritance from our heavenly Father when

776. John 14:2-3.
777. John 14:19.
778. 1 Cor. 15:53-54.

Jesus returns and sets up His kingdom on the earth. Our inheritance is established through our relationship with God the Father as His children. We are first born into the family of God, which means we are sons of God and no longer orphans. And second, when we were born again, we received the Spirit of adoption which means we will be placed in positions of authority within God's royal family to rule and reign with Jesus forever and ever.

Reigning with Jesus begins following the marriage supper of the Lamb. Jesus will return to earth with His bride and the kingdoms of this world shall become the kingdoms of our God and of His Christ. And we shall rule and reign with Jesus for one thousand years and that will complete the "week of redemption." During our millennial reign with the Lord Jesus over the entire world there will be no wars and the world will enjoy peace and prosperity. And the glory of the knowledge of God shall fill the earth as the waters cover the sea.

The one thousand year reign of the Lord Jesus and His bride begins with the devil being bound and cast into the bottomless pit for the duration of thousand years. In other words the powers of darkness will be confined to prison and the glorious light of Jesus Christ and His bride will release the inhabitants of the earth from the bondage of darkness and deception. And the glorious light of Jesus will illuminate the world.

At the conclusion of the millennial reign with Jesus there will be a new heaven and a new earth. There will also be a New Jerusalem, and in that city there will be no need of the sun or moon because the glory of God and the brilliance of the Lamb of God shall illuminate it. It will be a city of eternal peace, blessedness, and righteousness. "The sufferings of this present time are not worthy *to be compared* with the glory which shall be revealed in us."[779] In light of the hope of glory all believers must have their lamps burning and sufficient oil in preparation for meeting the very soon coming of the Lord Jesus! After all you have been through in this world you sure do not want to miss out on being at the marriage supper of the Lamb and entering into the glorious future that our heavenly Father has prepared for us! But never forget that the hope of glory is only possible because of what Jesus accomplished through His death, burial, resurrection, and ascension.

---

779. Rom. 8:18.

CHAPTER 8

Take Up Your Cross

"Then He said to *them* all, 'If anyone desires to come after Me, let him deny himself, and take up his cross daily, and follow Me. For whoever desires to save his life will lose it, but whoever loses his life for My sake will save it.'" (Luke 9:23-24)

"Now all things *are* of God, who has reconciled us to Himself through Jesus Christ, and has given us the ministry of reconciliation, that is, that God was in Christ reconciling the world to Himself, not imputing their trespasses to them, and has committed to us the word of reconciliation." (2 Corinthians 5:18-19)

IT IS BY FAITH in Jesus Christ and what He accomplished through His death on the cross, His burial, resurrection, and ascension, that we have access to God's provisions for our salvation. Our personal salvation unites us in a covenant relationship with God, our heavenly Father, and the Lord Jesus. That not only secures our eternal destiny but also empowers us to live holy and endure suffering for His sake as we daily bear our own cross. In previous chapters we have discussed in considerable detail what Jesus accomplished on our behalf through bearing His cross, but now we turn our attention to what it means for each of us to deny ourselves and daily take up our cross and follow Him. Jesus said, "If anyone desires to come after Me, let him deny himself, and take up his cross daily, and follow Me. For whoever desires to save his life will lose it, but whoever loses his life for My sake will save it."[780]

In this chapter we will discuss three different applications for experiencing what it means to deny yourself and take up your cross and follow Jesus. First, we will discuss the cross and the old man. The cross is a place of death, and all believers must "put to death your members which are on the earth: fornication, uncleanness, passion, evil desire, and covetousness, which is idolatry. Because of these things the wrath of God is coming upon the sons of disobedience,"[781] Second, the cross is a place of suffering, and all followers of Jesus must endure suffering through the chastening of the Lord. "For whom the LORD loves He chastens and scourges every son whom He receives." [782] And third, our discussion will focus on the cross and forgiveness. When we suffer injustice and personal injury, we must deny ourselves the privilege of vengeance, because vengeance belongs to the Lord.[783] We overcome evil with good, by turning the other cheek and forgiving the offender. "If you do not forgive men their trespasses, neither will your Father forgive your trespasses."[784] We once were disobedient and by nature children of wrath. But through the power of the cross we escape God's wrath and become partakers of His divine nature. Therefore, you are to "be renewed in the spirit of your mind, and that

---

780. Luke 9:23-24.
781. Col. 3:5-6.
782. Heb. 12:6.
783. Rom. 12:19-21.
784. Matt. 6:15.

you put on the new man which was created according to God, in true righteousness and holiness."[785]

The Cross and the Old Man:

It is helpful to keep in mind that you did not choose Jesus, but He chose you.[786] In other words, you are the object of God's love and compassion and were chosen in Christ before the foundation of the world.[787] Therefore, when Jesus was crucified, you were in Him, and thus you were also crucified. You have publicly confessed your union with Jesus Christ through water baptism.[788] You can now stand in any court and testify, "I have been crucified with Christ; it is no longer I who live, but Christ lives in me; and the *life* which I now live in the flesh I live by faith in the Son of God, who loved me and gave Himself for me."[789] Thus, if anyone *is* in Christ, *he is* a new creation; old things have passed away; behold, all things have become new."[790]

The reality is that God already sees you as glorified, because He has fulfilled every legal requirement for your glorification. But as believers you and I with the help of the Holy Spirit, must take the personal responsibility to "put off the old man with his deeds and put on the new *man* who is renewed in knowledge according to the image of Him who created him."[791] And "present ourselves to God as being alive from the dead, and our members *as* instruments of righteousness

---

785. Eph. 4:23-24.
786. John 15:6.
787. Eph. 1:4.
788. Rom. 6:5.
789. Gal. 2:20.
790. 2 Cor. 5:17.
791. Col. 3:9-10.

to God.[792] "We are debtors—not to the flesh, to live according to the flesh. For if you live according to the flesh you will die; but if by the Spirit you put to death the deeds of the body, you will live."[793] Putting to death the deeds of the body is the function of bearing our personal cross.

The cross you are called to bear isn't simply about you and your stuff. No! God desires to demonstrate the wisdom of the cross through you and me to the unseen rulers of this world. In other words, the cross is not all about you, but also about God's plan that is much bigger than you and me. "Jesus said to His disciples, 'If anyone desires to come after Me, let him deny himself, and take up his cross, and follow Me.'"[794] Of course God wants to bless and prosper every person, but the devil is an adversary who opposes God and the people of God. The devil's plan is to kill, steal, and destroy.[795] But it is God's nature and purpose to give life and to give it abundantly. Therefore, it is only reasonable and congruent with God's nature that His children express the same nature and purpose as their Father. When we are born again, we are reconciled together with God our Creator and heavenly Father.[796] Also at the new birth we receive the Holy Spirit and old things pass away, and we become new persons in Christ.[797] However, we remain in our same body until resurrection day when our corruptible and mortal bodies will be changed in a moment. On that day our corruptible body will put on incorruption and our mortal body will put on immortality.[798] But until resurrection

792. Rom. 6:13.
793. Rom. 8:12-14.
794. Matt. 16:24.
795. John 10:10.
796. 2 Cor. 5:18-19.
797. 2 Cor. 5:17.
798. 1 Cor. 15:53-54.

day we continue to live in a body of flesh that is sinful by nature.[799] When we receive Jesus as our Lord and Savior our spirit is born again or anew, our minds must be renewed by the word of God. But until resurrection day our bodily urges, compulsion and appetites that do not express the nature and purpose of God must be crucified. We cannot let those bodily urges and compulsions be the factors that express our lifestyle. We must put off the old man by daily crucifying the urges and compulsions of the flesh and "put on the new *man* who is renewed in knowledge according to the image of Him who created him, where there is neither Greek nor Jew, circumcised nor uncircumcised, barbarian, Scythian, slave *nor* free, but Christ *is* all and in all."[800]

There are two aspects to our righteousness: First, is the righteousness of God which is accounted to us through the judicial process of our justification. Walter Elwell states, "Righteousness is that attribute by which God's nature is seen to be the eternally perfect standard of what is right."[801] We cannot attain unto God's standard of righteousness, so, the Father takes the righteousness of Jesus and applies it to our account, and thus declares us to be righteous or in right standing before Him. And the second aspect of our righteousness consists of our right deeds or right actions. Because we are born with a sin nature it is not possible to meet God's standard of righteousness. The Scriptures defines our righteousness as follows; "But we are all like an unclean *thing*, And all our righteousnesses *are* like filthy rags...."[802] But after being justified the Holy Spirit comes to live in our hearts, which constitutes being born again or regenerated.

799. Rom. 7:18.
800. Col. 3:8-11.
801. Elwell, *Evangelical Dictionary of Theology*, 1034.
802. Isa. 64:6a.

The Holy Spirit gives us a new nature and helps us live according to God's nature or standard.

The challenge all believers face is the fact that we presently live in a body infected with sin. This body has sinful appetites or urges that Scriptures define as our "old man." "For we know that the law is spiritual, but I am carnal, sold under sin. For what I am doing, I do not understand. For what I will to do, that I do not practice; but what I hate, that I do."[803] Even though we are "born again" and our spirit is regenerated, we still live in the same body of flesh, which is yet to be saved, that is, it will be changed in a moment on resurrection morning. In a twinkling of an eye this corruptible body will put on incorruption, and this mortal will put on immortality.[804] All of us face the reality there are occasions when we say or do things that cause us to wonder—"Why did I do such a stupid or foolish thing?" We did not intend to say or do what we did, but it happened because of the sinful wretchedness of our flesh. And in desperate humility we cry out saying, "O wretched man that I am! Who will deliver me from this body of death? I thank God--through Jesus Christ our Lord!"[805] Glory be to God, we are no longer prisoners to the bondage of sin, because the wages of sin is death, and we have already died, because we were crucified with Christ. Jesus paid our sin penalty and we are now empowered to fulfill our responsibility as children of God by repenting before the Lord and asking Him and those we have offended to forgive us. "If we confess our sins, He is faithful and just to forgive us *our* sins and to cleanse us from all unrighteousness."[806]

---

803. Rom. 7:14-15.
804. 1 Cor. 15:52-53.
805. Rom. 7:24-25a.
806. 1 John 1:9.

Far too many believers live in spiritual weakness because of their misunderstanding of righteousness. In other words, they sin and repent, but live under a cloud of condemnation and shame because they feel like failures in as much as they repeated their sin. We are not condoning a sinful lifestyle, but character development takes time plus painful disciplines. Few people successfully ride a bicycle the first time they try. But they keep trying until they can ride without stress. And so, it is with intrenched sinful personal character habits. After we are born again we will stumble and fall a few times or many times before we develop a Christ-like character. But even in our stumbling and falling we stand as righteous before God.

The message of the cross is that we are accounted righteous on the same basis as Abraham was accounted righteous. "For what does the Scripture say? 'Abraham believed God, and it was accounted to him for righteousness.'"[807] Think of your righteousness according to the terms of the following Scripture.

> But when the kindness and the love of God our Savior toward man appeared, **not by works of righteousness which we have done, but according to His mercy He saved us**, through the washing of regeneration and renewing of the Holy Spirit, whom He poured out on us abundantly through Jesus Christ our Savior, **that having been justified by His grace** we should become heirs according to the hope of eternal life. (Titus 3:4-7, emphasis mine).

---

807. Gen. 15:6; Rom. 4:3.

When we repent of our sin and ask Jesus to be our Savior and Lord, the Father forgives our sin and remembers it no more. Then He takes the righteousness of Jesus and applies it to our personal account. "For He (*God the Father*) made Him (*Jesus*) who knew no sin *to be* sin for us, that **we might become the righteousness of God in Him.**"[808] (Emphasis mine). With reference to this Scripture, R. C. H. Lenski states, "This is one of the most tremendous statements written by Paul's pen. It is so tremendous because it so completely and in such a striking form reveals what God has done for us."[809] Lenski further states,

> God made Christ sin ὑπὲρ ἡμῶν by charging all that is "sin" in us against him, by letting him bear all this burden with all its guilt and penalty "in our stead" in order to deliver us. It sounds incredible that God should have done this with his own *sinless* Son. Because it is so astounding Paul puts it in this astounding way. But it is fact, God *did* this.[810]

The message of the cross is that Jesus has made every provision for our salvation, our righteousness, and has given us the Holy Spirit to help us be transformed in His likeness. On the cross, sin was condemned and thus no longer has dominion over you.[811] Through faith in Jesus Christ and by the grace of God, believers in Jesus are justified or declared righteous.[812] "*There is* therefore now no condemnation to

---

808. 2 Cor. 5:21.

809. R. C. H. Lenski, *The Interpretation of St. Paul's First and Second Epistle to the Corinthians* (Minneapolis, MN: Augsburg Publishing House, 1963), 1051.

810. Ibid., 1053.

811. Rom. 8:3-4.

812. Titus 3:4-7.

those who are in Christ Jesus, who do not walk according to the flesh, but according to the Spirit."[813] Our responsibility is to know our true identity according to God's terms and not according to the terms of the world. By denying ourselves and daily taking up our cross and applying the cross to our character, that is by crucifying or putting to death our sinful appetites, our character is transformed. Denying ourselves and daily taking up the cross is the process of taking off the old man and putting on the new man. That is a painful business that extends over our lifetime. We are further instructed to put on the breastplate of righteousness in order to defend and protect our heart against those who would condemn us or call into question our standing of righteousness before God. "Yet in all these things we are more than conquerors through Him who loved us."[814]

The Cross and the Chastening of the Lord:

There are occasions when we do wrong things and then suffer the consequences. We know we were wrong and deserve those consequences. But Job was a man that was "blameless and upright, and one who feared God and shunned evil."[815] Job suddenly suffered the loss of his children, his wealth, his health, and his wife told him to "Curse God and die!"[816] His three friends falsely accused him of hidden sin.[817] Yet Job remained steadfast in faith even as he suffered from boils over his entire body.[818] Through Job, God was demonstrating to Satan and the powers of darkness that there are individuals who will trust

813. Rom. 8:1-2.
814. Rom. 8:37.
815. Job 1:1.
816. Job 2:9.
817. Job 10:6-14.
818. Job 2:7.

the Lord not just in prosperity, but even through great suffering and personal loss. That reality has not changed over redemptive history. Today the Lord gives grace to make all to see what is the fellowship of the mystery hidden in God "to the intent that now the manifold wisdom of God might be made known by the church to principalities and powers in heavenly places according to the eternal purpose which He accomplished in Christ our Lord."[819]

Consider Joseph, the son of Jacob. He was hated by his brothers and sold into slavery. His father had given him a special coat of many colors and as a result he had probably expressed some arrogance and maybe spoke unwisely, but he surely didn't deserve being hated and sold into slavery. However, when we look back over the entirety of Joseph's life experiences, we agree that those experiences were painful and seemed unfair, but "God meant it for good."[820] What Joseph experienced helps you and me better understand the paradox of the cross, and the godly wisdom behind necessity for the cross that we are to take up daily as we follow Jesus. "Now no chastening seems to be joyful for the present, but painful; nevertheless, afterward it yields the peaceable fruit of righteousness to those who have been trained by it."[821]

Joseph's painful experiences were disciplines that contributed to the development of his godly character, preparing him to carry the weight of responsibility necessary to lead the land of Egypt through seven years of famine. His leadership was so successful that it even contributed to the survival for his own father and brethren. Earlier, Joseph had pleaded with his brothers not to sell him into slavery.[822]

819. Eph. 3:9-11.
820. Gen. 50:20.
821. Heb. 12:11.
822. Gen. 42:21.

But they refused to listen or relent. Hence, he was sold into slavery, and after some years of faithfully serving his Egyptian slave master, he was falsely accused and thrown into prison.[823] And there in prison "they hurt his feet with fetters, he was laid in irons."[824] During all those times Joseph was experiencing the chastening of the Lord, not because he was a bad person, but because God had greater things in store for him. God was unfolding His plan of redemption that He had originally launched through a covenant with Joseph's great-grandfather Abraham. So, Joseph was chosen by God to be a major contributor to the ongoing revelation of the kingdom of God on the earth. Therefore, God needed to train Joseph to be His ambassador over Egypt.

There were occasions when Joseph probably felt abused, forgotten, and may have experienced discouragement. Submitting our life to the Lordship of Jesus Christ will bring you and me into experiencing the cross and the disciplines of the Lord. Therefore, "consider Him who endured such hostility from sinners against Himself, lest you become weary and discouraged in your souls."[825] Solomon expresses the wisdom of God by stating, "My son, do not despise the chastening of the LORD, nor detest His correction; for whom the LORD loves He corrects, just as a father the son *in whom* he delights."[826] As Joseph's life unfolded, he learned that God had orchestrated his experiences. He understood that the grace of God had made his brothers hatred and misdeeds the means of Israel's salvation.[827] God continues to

---

823. Gen. 39:20.
824. Psa. 105:18.
825. Heb. 12:3.
826. Prov. 3:11-12.
827. Carl Friedrich Keil and Franz Delitzsch, *Commentary on the Old Testament*, vol. 1 (Peabody, MA: Hendrickson, 1996), 265.

express His saving grace by choosing you and me to now serve as His ambassadors in this culture that has lost its way. The Apostle Peter understood this when he said, "Beloved, do not think it strange concerning the fiery trial which is to try you, as though some strange thing happened to you; but rejoice to the extent that you partake of Christ's sufferings, that when His glory is revealed, you may also be glad with exceeding joy."[828] George H. Guthrie states, "The rationale for taking the Lord's discipline seriously and taking courage when facing His rebuke has to do with His motive of love.... Such training is only given to legitimate children."[829] Therefore, "If you endure chastening, God deals with you as with sons; for what son is there whom a father does not chasten?"[830]

Man was created by God and given "dominion over the fish of the sea, over the birds of the air, and over the cattle, over all the earth and over every creeping thing that creeps on the earth."[831] It was God's intention that mankind would rule over the earth, rather than being slaves under the dominion of the "god of this age".[832] Our bondage and death is rooted in our sinful condition that we inherited from our father, Adam. The broken or sinful nature that we inherited from Adam not only infects our whole being, but also, nature itself groans under the same bondage.[833] The point is that we were created to be rulers over our environment because our Creator "put all things in subjection under his (*man's*) feet."[834] (Emphasis mine). "But now we

---

828. 1 Peter 4:12-13.

829. George H. Guthrie, *Hebrews: The Application Commentary* (Grand Rapids, MI: Zondervan, 1998), 401.

830. Heb. 12:7.

831. Gen 1:26.

832. 2 Cor. 4:4.

833. Rom. 5:12, 8:22-23.

834. Heb. 2:8.

do not yet see all things put under him (*mankind*). But we see Jesus, who was made a little lower than the angels, for the suffering of death crowned with glory and honor, that He, by the grace of God, might taste death for everyone."[835] (Emphasis mine).

Jesus is our primary example of having to endure the chastening of the Lord. Jesus never sinned yet died on the cross for you and me. What can we learn from His exemplary life? First, He was conceived in the womb of the Virgin Mary by the overshadowing of the Holy Spirit.[836] This was unlike you and me who were conceived by the will of the flesh and needed to be born again of the Holy Spirit. Jesus was born of the Holy Spirit and lived a sinless life.[837] Second, at age twelve He journeyed from Nazareth to Jerusalem with His parents to celebrate the Feast of Passover. And when Joseph and Mary traveled back towards Nazareth a day's journey, they discovered that Jesus was not in the crowd with them. They returned to Jerusalem and after three days found Jesus in the temple "sitting in the midst of the teachers, both listening to them and asking them questions. And all who heard Him were astonished at His understanding and answers."[838] In other words Jesus was brilliant even in his childhood. Third, He not only astonished the teachers, but He is also our Creator. "All things were made through Him, and without Him nothing was made that was made."[839] "And He is before all things, and in Him all things consist."[840] No other individual on earth has ever had that accomplishment or depth of background. And fourth, even though Jesus

---

835. Heb. 2:9.
836. Luke 1:35.
837. John 3:3, 7.
838. Luke 2:46-47.
839. John 3:1.
840. Col. 1:17.

was holy, harmless, undefiled, and separate from sinners, He had to learn obedience by the things He suffered.[841] Obedience is not simply a fact or formula, nor is it a gift of the Holy Spirit. Obedience must be experienced by surrendering our will totally to the will of the Father, regardless of personal cost or pain. And Jesus Himself prayed three times, "O My Father, if it is possible, let this cup pass from Me; nevertheless, not as I will, but as You *will*."[842] Jesus had to learn by experience what it means to bear your own cross. Jesus had to learn obedience just as Joseph, you, and I, must learn by experience the meaning and value of obedience. "To obey is better than sacrifice."[843]

Obedience in the face of suffering is demonstrated by the example of Jesus's Apostles. It wasn't long after Jesus' ascension that the ministry of the Apostles came into conflict with the Jewish religious leaders in Jerusalem. The Apostles were brought before the Jewish council and beaten, then commanded not to speak in the name of Jesus. "So they departed from the presence of the council, rejoicing that they were counted worthy to suffer shame for His name."[844] Ray Steadman states, "Discomfort, hardship and deprivations, borne for the sake of Christ, are viewed as privileges and blessings, sent by a loving Father to prepare us to be worthy heirs of the incomparable glories yet to come."[845] "But when we are judged, we are chastened by the Lord, that we may not be condemned with the world."[846] Our chastening is not a sign of God's displeasure, but a sign that He

---

841. Heb. 5:8.

842. Matt. 26:39

843. 1 Sam. 15:22.

844. Acts 5:41.

845. Ray C. Stedman, *Hebrews*, The IVP New Testament Commentary Series (Westmont, IL: IVP Academic, 1992), Heb 12:4–13.

846. 1 Cor. 11:32.

regards us as genuine children. "For whom the Lord loves He chastens and scourges every son He receives."[847]

Discipline not only comes to those who have violated their God given responsibilities, but also to all who are being trained for kingdom assignments. Steadman states, "Many Christians today have testified that God got their attention only after some severe trial or circumstance that came upon them!"[848] "But if you are without chastening, of which all have become partakers, then you are illegitimate and not sons."[849] The chastening of the Lord flows out of His love for us and His commitment to our eternal salvation. When we understand the significance of the glorious purposes of our heavenly Father we will "glory in tribulations, knowing that tribulation produces perseverance; and perseverance, character; and character, hope. Now hope does not disappoint, because the love of God has been poured out in our hearts by the Holy Spirit who was given to us."[850] Bruce Barton states, "Submission to God's discipline means not trying to wriggle out of it by making excuses or hardening our hearts; instead, it means allowing the discipline to drive us to our knees before God so that he can teach us the lessons he has for us."[851] We tend to resist the disciplines necessary to transform our character, because we, like Peter, "are not mindful of the things of God, but the things of men."[852] The chastening of the Lord is painful, but afterwards yields

---

847. Heb. 12:6.

848. Stedman, *Hebrews*, Heb 12:4–13.

849. Heb. 12:8.

850. Rom. 5:3-5.

851. Bruce B. Barton et al., *Hebrews*, Life Application Bible Commentary (Wheaton, IL: Tyndale House Publishers, 1997), 210–211.

852. Matt. 16:23-25.

the peaceful fruit of righteousness and enables you and me to be partakers of God's holiness if we are trained by it.[853]

Esau is an example of one who did not endure the disciplines of the Lord, and in his hour of testing he sold his birthright for a bowl of vegetables."[854] Surely, there will be occasions when we will become exhausted and discouraged, but we must consider Jesus as our ultimate example: "who for the joy that was set before Him endured the cross, despising the shame, and has sat down at the right hand of God."[855] The Lord has prepared a glorious future for His redeemed family, but it is he who endures to the end that shall be saved.[856] Therefore we are exhorted to "strengthen the hands which hang down, and the feeble knees, and make straight paths for your feet, so that what is lame may not be *dislocated*, but rather be healed."[857] Earlier the writer of the Book of Hebrews exhorts us by saying, "Do not cast away your confidence, which has great reward. For you have need of endurance, so that after you have done the will of God, you may receive the promise."[858] Esau did not endure, but under his exhaustion and the pressure of his own appetite, he sold his birthright, and thereby fell short of the grace of God. He forfeited his inheritance and the blessings it contained even though he afterwards sought it diligently with tears.[859]

We are further exhorted not to "receive the grace of God in vain. For He says: 'In an acceptable time I have heard you, and in the day of salvation I have helped you.' Behold, now *is* the accepted time;

853. Heb. 12:10-11.
854. Heb. 12:12-13.
855. Hen. 12:2.
856. Matt. 24:13; Mk. 13:13.
857. Heb. 12:12-13.
858. Heb. 10:35-36.
859. Heb. 12:15-17.

behold, now *is* the day of salvation."[860] Aren't you glad that Jesus didn't refuse to meet His appointment for His crucifixion and make an excuse for some more convenient time. To experience the cross is not a "joyful but a painful experience; nevertheless, afterward it yields the peaceful fruit of righteousness to those who are trained by it."[861] "We preach Christ crucified, to the Jews a stumbling block and to the Greeks foolishness, but to those who are called, both Jews and Greeks, Christ the power of God and the wisdom of God."[862]

It is amazing how much anger, resentment, and bitterness can distort our sense reality and blind us to the value of our birthright as children of God. Therefore, we are to be as wise as serpents and harmless as doves.[863] "Do all things without complaining and disputing, that you may become blameless and harmless, children of God without fault in the midst of a crooked and perverse generation, among whom you shine as lights in the world."[864] It is when we comport with these admonishments in submission to the chastenings of the Lord that we Christians reveal the meaning and value of the cross and the birthright that is ours to the culture around us. It is then, that those around us see our good works and glorify our Father which is in heaven.[865]

The Cross and Forgiveness:

Jesus had endured four trials and in the fifth and final trial Pilate the Roman Governor of Jerusalem thoroughly examined Jesus again

---

860. 2 Cor. 6:1-2.
861. Heb. 12:11.
862. 1 Cor. 1 23.
863. Matt. 10:16.
864. Phil. 2:14-15.
865. Matt. 6:15.

and declared, "I find no fault in Him."[866] Yet the crowd continued to cry out saying, "Crucify Him, crucify Him!" Under the political pressure exerted against Pilate's better judgment, he delivered Jesus to them to be crucified.[867] And there after several hours having been severely beaten and bloody beyond recognition and hanging on the cross "Jesus said, 'Father, forgive them, for they do not know what they do.'"[868] At the cross-man's sins are forgiven and God's wrath is propitiated. To the best of my understanding the cross and forgiveness are very, very serious issues regarding human relationships. Because, when Jesus asked the Father to forgive His accusers and executioners, He was offering each of them an opportunity to start over in their relationship with Him. What an awesome offer! Lewis B. Smedes states, "The miracle of forgiving is the creation of a new beginning. It does not always take away the hurt. It does not deny the past injury. It merely refuses to let them stand in the way of a new start."[869] With Jesus' words "Father forgive them," He was offering all sinners including you and me an opportunity to have a fresh start with our Creator against whom we have all sinned. Smedes continues, "Forgiveness does not deny the past; it can only create a new future."[870]

When we deny ourselves and daily take up our cross as a lifestyle, we enter a shared pain with God the Father, and what Jesus experienced at Calvary. When we confess our sin, the Father stands ready and willing to forgive our sin and cleanse us of all unrighteousness.[871]

866. John 18:38, 19:4, 19:6.
867. John 19:16.
868. Luke 23:34.
869. Lewis B. Smedes, *Can It Be All Right When Everything Is Wrong?* (Wheaton, Il: Harold Shaw Publishing, 1999), 55.
870. Ibid.
871. 1 John 1:9.

Even though we have sinned and fallen short of the glory of God, He stands ready to forgive and start over. He longs to be our Father and Savior and has made every provision to have communion with each of us. Therefore, do not allow the enemy of your soul to pour condemnation on you and shut yourself up to misunderstanding and unbelief. "Come boldly to the throne of grace, that we may obtain mercy and find grace to help in time of need."[872]

When God created mankind, He granted man the dignity of a free will. Man could choose to obey God or disobey God. God's standard of righteousness by which we distinguish between right and wrong or good and evil is established by His infallible and immutable nature. God says, "I am the Lord, I do not change."[873] Unlike God, we fallible individuals do change. Sometimes we make good choices and sometimes we make bad choices. Hence, our morality is determined by the choices we make. The hope of our salvation rests upon the reality that through Jesus' sacrificial death on the cross, God has provided His forgiveness for our wrong choices, our sin. "In Him we have redemption through His blood, the forgiveness of sins, according to the riches of His grace which He made to abound toward us in all wisdom and prudence."[874] In other words, Forgiveness is God's antidote to offences and sin according to Lee Bowman.[875] The fact is that forgiveness is a central issue to maintaining healthy relationships with fallible people, and fallible people are the only kind of people living in your family and this world. L. Gregory Jones states,

---

872. Heb. 4:16.

873. Mal. 3:6; Heb. 13:8.

874. Eph. 1:7-8.

875. John Loren, Paula Sandford, and Lew Bowman, *Choosing Forgiveness: Turning from Guilt, Bitterness, and Resentment Toward a Life of Wholeness and Peace* (Lake Mary, FL: Charisma House, 2007), 2.

"Forgiveness indicates the ongoing priority of the Church's task to offer the endlessly creative and gratuitous gift of new life in the face of sin and brokenness."[876] Therefore, "Be kind to one another, tenderhearted, forgiving one another, just as God in Christ forgave you."[877]

Stuart K. Weber states, "The Bible makes it clear that there is nothing we can do to merit God's judicial forgiveness, but that it is given freely (e.g., Rom. 5:6–8; Eph. 2:8–9)."[878] Jesus teaches us to ask God to "forgive us our debts" or sins.[879] The Apostle John teaches, "If we confess our sins, He is faithful and just to forgive us *our* sins and to cleanse us from all unrighteousness."[880] Jesus said, "For if you forgive men their trespasses, your heavenly Father will also forgive you. But if you do not forgive men their trespasses, neither will your Father forgive your trespasses."[881] Weber continues by stating,

> One does not gain forgiveness by forgiving. **But a person evidences his or her own forgiveness by forgiving others**. Since this is family forgiveness, our sense of forgiveness is denied us when we deny forgiveness to others. **As God's children, we are commanded to be forgiving**. When we fail to forgive, we reap the consequences of spiritual and moral defeat.[882] (Emphasis mine).

---

876. L. Gregory Jones, *Embodying Forgiveness: A Theological Analysis* (Grand Rapids, MI: Wm. B. Eerdmans Publishing Co., 1995), 5.

877. Eph. 4:32.

878. Stuart K. Weber, *Matthew*, vol. 1, Holman New Testament Commentary (Nashville, TN: Broadman & Holman Publishers, 2000), 82.

879. Matt. 6:12.

880. 1 John 1:9.

881. Matt. 6:14-15.

882. Weber, *Matthew*, 82–83.

Forgiveness opens the door to the possibility of enemies becoming friends. The issue at stake in this discussion clearly teaches that forgiveness is a prerequisite to reconciliation. Ladd states, "Reconciliation is necessary between two parties when something has occurred to disrupt fellowship with God."[883] However, forgiveness does not guarantee reconciliation, but it does release one from the past and opens the door to the possibility of a new start of a harmonious relationship broken by sin. At the cross, "God was in Christ reconciling the world to Himself, not imputing their trespasses to them."[884] And God has given us, the Church, the "ministry of reconciliation."[885] Lenski states, "By means of this ministry which has been placed into our hands by God, Paul says, God is doing this wondrous work, bringing reconciliation and pardon from sin to the world, i.e., 'to them,' the individuals in the world."[886] In other words, Jesus Christ shedding His blood and dying on the cross as our substitute and for the remission of our sin is the means of God's reconciliation with repentant sinners. Ladd continues, "Because God has effected a work of reconciliation for them, people are in turn to respond in loving submission to the gracious overture of a loving God and so be reconciled to God."[887]

All this discussion has a practical application for each of us personally. We were born with a sin nature. That means no one had to teach you and me to sin, we simply sinned against God because it was our nature by birth. We lived as sinners without God, without hope,

883. Ladd, *A Theology*, 492.

884. 2 Cor. 5:19.

885. 2 Cor. 5:18.

886. R. C. H. Lenski, *The Interpretation of St. Paul's First and Second Epistle to the Corinthians* (Minneapolis, MN: Augsburg Publishing House, 1963), 1043.

887. Ladd, *A Theology*, 494.

and full of fear. But God so loved us that He sent His only begotten Son into the world to redeem and make possible the reconciliation of lost sinners back to Himself. Jesus at the appointed time totally surrendered His will to the will of the Father and laid His sinless life down in our place on the cross for the remission of sin, not only for us but for the whole world. In other words, we were alienated from God by a sin nature and had a sin debt that we did not have the will nor resource to pay. But Jesus, the good Shepherd, was willing to pay our debt, which He did not owe. At the cross, man's sins are forgiven, and God's wrath is propitiated. "God demonstrates His own love toward us, in that while we were still sinners, Christ died for us."[888] Jesus crucified and risen from the dead, having paid our sin debt, made forgiveness of sin and reconciliation with the Father possible to all who would repent and call on the Lord. "If you confess with your mouth the Lord Jesus and believe in your heart that God has raised Him from the dead, you will be saved."[889] "For 'whoever calls on the name of the LORD shall be saved.'"[890]

We are not only forgiven and reconciled with our heavenly Father, but we receive the Holy Spirit of promise who is the guarantee of our inheritance.[891] He is the "Spirit of adoption by whom we cry out, Abba, Father."[892] "You are no longer a slave, but a son, and if a son, then an heir of God through Christ."[893] Gordon Fee states, "The Spirit is God's abiding presence, but He does not eliminate our humanity;

---

888. Rom. 5:8.
889. Rom. 10:9.
890. Rom. 10:13.
891. Eph. 1:13-14.
892. Rom. 8:15.
893. Gal. 4:7.

He has redeemed it and now works through it."[894] "Then Jesus said to *them* all, 'If anyone desires to come after Me, let him deny himself, and take up his cross daily, and follow Me. For whoever desires to save his life will lose it, but whoever loses his life for My sake will save it.'"[895] We are no longer enemies and alienated from God, but "we are ambassadors for Christ, as though God were pleading through us: we implore *you* on Christ's behalf, be reconciled to God."[896] We now plead with others to be reconciled with God because we are not only sons of God, but commissioned to proclaim the gospel of the kingdom of God as God's ambassadors in this world. "Therefore, as *the* elect of God, holy and beloved, put on tender mercies, kindness, humility, meekness, longsuffering; bearing with one another, and forgiving one another, if anyone has a complaint against another; even as Christ forgave you, so you also *must do*."[897] Jesus said, "By this My Father is glorified, that you bear much fruit; so you will be My disciples."[898]

Summary:

The discussion in this book has centered around the atonement and what Jesus accomplished for you and me through His death, burial, resurrection, and ascension. But this final chapter focuses on three aspects of what it means to deny oneself, take up your cross daily and follow Jesus. The first aspect of this chapter addresses "the cross and the old man." When we are born-again, our spirit is

---

894. Gordon D. Fee, *God's Empowering Presence: The Holy Spirit in the Letters of Paul* (Peabody, MA: Hendrickson Publishers, Inc., 1999), 567.

895. Luke 9:23-24.

896. 2 Cor. 5:20.

897. Col. 3:12-13.

898. John 15:8.

regenerated, we are reconciled with our heavenly Father, united with the Lord Jesus, and the Holy Spirit comes to live in our bodily temple.[899] Our soul which includes our mind, will, and emotions must be renewed and transformed by bringing them into an alignment with the word of God.[900] That is a part of Biblical discipleship. But our body, as often described in Scripture as "flesh", will not be saved until resurrection day. Meanwhile it is wired with sinful urges, compulsions, and appetites which must be crucified. "Therefore, brethren, we are debtors--not to the flesh, to live according to the flesh. For if you live according to the flesh you will die; but if by the Spirit you put to death the deeds of the body, you will live."[901] We must "put off, concerning your former conduct, the old man which grows corrupt according to the deceitful lusts, and be renewed in the spirit of your mind, and that you put on the new man which was created according to God, in true righteousness and holiness."[902] "But God forbid that I should boast except in the cross of our Lord Jesus Christ, by whom the world has been crucified to me, and I to the world."[903]

The second aspect of what it means to deny oneself, take up your cross daily and follow Jesus focuses on "the cross and the chastening of the Lord." The chastening of the Lord is not because of His displeasure. Rather, it is evidence of His Fatherly love for us. "'For whom the LORD loves He chastens, and scourges every son whom He receives.' If you endure chastening, God deals with you as with sons; for what son is there whom a father does not chasten?"[904] The Lord

---

899. 2 Cor. 5:17.
900. Rom. 12:1-2.
901. Rom. 8:12-13.
902. Eph 4:22-24.
903. Gal. 6:14.
904. Heb. 12:6-7.

has awesome things in store for you and His chastening contributes to the transformation of your character in preparation for the weight of responsibility and anointing you will carry. "Now no chastening seems to be joyful for the present, but painful; nevertheless, afterward it yields the peaceable fruit of righteousness to those who have been trained by it."[905] Therefore, "do not despise the chastening of the Lord, nor be discouraged when you are rebuked by Him."[906] "But rejoice to the extent that you partake of Christ's sufferings, that when His glory is revealed, you may also be glad with exceeding joy."[907]

The third and final aspect of what it means to deny oneself, take up your cross daily and follow Jesus focuses on "the cross and forgiveness." All of us rejoice when we experience the forgiveness of sins, and the blessedness of being reconciled together with our heavenly Father. And we should celebrate the reality of being liberated from guilt, shame, and "delivered from the power of darkness and conveyed into the kingdom of the Son of His love."[908] "Stand fast therefore in the liberty by which Christ has made us free, and do not be entangled again with a yoke of bondage."[909] Now that we are members of the family of God we can shout; "Behold what manner of love the Father has bestowed on us, that we should be called children of God! Therefore, the world does not know us, because it did not know Him."[910]

But as the children of God and disciples of Jesus Christ, we are expected to grow strong in the grace of God, to the extent that we

---

905. Heb. 12:11.
906. Heb. 12:5.
907. 1 Peter 4:13.
908. Col. 1:13.
909. Gal. 5:1.
910. 1 John 3:1.

digest the meat of the word of God and mature into the "stature of the fullness Christ."[911] Because God "has given to us the ministry of reconciliation."[912] The prerequisite to reconciliation is forgiveness. Jesus teaches us by His words and lifestyle to be forgiving. There on the cross all bloody and shamed, He looked at His accusers and executioners and said, "Father forgive them for they do not know what they do."[913] Earlier Jesus had taught, "For if you forgive men their trespasses, your heavenly Father will also forgive you. But if you do not forgive men their trespasses, neither will your Father forgive your trespasses."[914] We find it hard to forgive another when they have injured us or when they are wrong and we know we are right. But Jesus is our example, and on the cross He said, "Father forgive them" even when He could have called down legions of angels to His defense.[915] At the cross we must surrender our will and say, "Father, not my will but your will be done." Denying ourselves, taking up our cross daily, and practicing forgiveness is a key to fulfilling our ministry of reconciliation and serving as His ambassadors.

911. Heb. 5:12-14; Eph. 4:13.
912. 2 Cor. 5:18.
913. Luke 23:34.
914. Matt. 6:14-15.
915. Matt. 26:53.

Selected Bibliography

Beckwith, Francis J., William Lane Craig, and J. P. Moreland, eds., *To Everyone An Answer: A Case for the Christian Worldview*. Downers Grove, IL: InterVarsity Press, 2004.

Billheimer, Paul E., *Destined for the Throne: How Spiritual Warfare Prepares the Bride of Christ for Her Eternal Destiny*, rev. ed., Bloomington, MN: Bethany House Publishers, 1996.

Block, Daniel I., *Covenant: The Framework of God's Grand Plan of Redemption*. Grand Rapids, MI: Baker Academic, 2021.

Bruce, F. F., *The Gospel of John & Epistles of John*. Grand Rapids, MI: William B. Eerdmans Publishing Company, 2001.

Conner, Kevin, *The Feasts of Israel*. Portland, OR: BT Publishing, 1980.

Conner, Kevin J., and Ken Malmin, *Interpreting the Scriptures: A Textbook on How to Interpret the Bible*. Portland, OR: BT Publishing, 1983.

Ellis, Larry D., *Forgiveness: Unleashing a Transformational Process*. Denver, CO: Adoration Publishing Company, 2010.

Elwell, Walter A., *Evangelical Dictionary of Theology: Second Edition*. Grand Rapids, MI: Baker Academic, 2001.

Erickson, Millard J., *Christian Theology.*, 2nd ed., Grand Rapids, MI: Baker Book House, 1998.

Fee, Gordon D., *Pauline Christology: An Exegetical-Theological Study*. Peabody, MA: Hendrickson Publications, Inc., 2007.

_____, Gordon D., *The First Epistle to the Corinthians: The New International Commentary on the New Testament*, Grand Rapids, MI: William B. Eerdmans Publishing Co., 1987.

Habershon, Ada R., *The Study of the Types*, Grand Rapids, MI: Kregel Publications, 1974.

Geisler, Norman L., *Systematic Theology, Volume Three: Sin, Salvation*. Minneapolis, MN: Bethany House Publishers, 2004.

Heiser, Michael S., *The Unseen Realm: Recovering the Supernatural Worldview of the Bible*. Bellingham, WA: Lexham Press, 2015.

Hill, Charles H., and Frank A. James, eds., *The Glory of the Atonement*. Downers Grove, Il: InterVarsity, 2004.

Horton, Michael, *Introducing Covenant Theology*. Grand Rapids, MI: Baker Books, 2006.

Jeffery, Steve, Michael Ovey, and Andrew Sach. *Pierced for Our Transgressions*. Wheaton, Il: Crossway, 2007.

Jones, L. Gregory, *Embodying Forgiveness: A Theological Analysis*. Grand Rapids, MI: Wm. B. Eerdmans Publishing Co., 1995

King, Paul L., *Come Up Higher: Rediscovering Throne Life: The Highest Christian Life for the 21st Century*. Tulsa, OK: One Seed Press, 2013.

Ladd, George Eldon. *A Theology of the New Testament*, rev. ed., Grand Rapids, MI: William B. Eerdmans Publishing Company, 1993.

_____, George Eldon, *Commentary on the Revelation*. Grand Rapids, MI: Eerdmans Publishing Co., 1972.

Lenski, R. C. H., *The Interpretation of St. Matthew's Gospel*. Minneapolis, MN: Augsburg Publishing House, 1961.

Moffitt, David M., *Rethinking the Atonement: New Perspectives on Jesus's Death, Resurrection, and Ascension*. Grand Rapids, MI: Baker Academic, 2022.

Moreland, J. P. and William Lane Craig, *Philosophical Foundations for a Christian Worldview.* Downers Grove, IL: InterVarsity Press, 2003.

Morris, Henry M., *The Genesis Record: A Scientific & Devotional Commentary on the Book of Beginnings.* Grand Rapids, MI: Baker Book House, 1976.

Morris, Leon, *The Apostolic Preaching of the Cross.* Grand Rapids, MI: William B. Eerdmans Publishing Co., 1965.

Mounce, Willian D., *Mounce's Complete Expository Dictionary of Old & New Testament Words.* Grand Rapids, MI: Zondervan, 2006.

Murray, Andrew, *The Holiest of All.* New Kensington, PA: Whitaker House, 1996.

Murray, John, *Redemption Accomplished and Applied.* Grand Rapids, MI: Wm. B. Eerdmans Publishing, 2015.

Packer, J. I., *Knowing God.* Downers Grove, IL: InterVarsity Press, 1993.

Packer, J. I., and Mark Denver, *In My Place He Stood: Celebrating the Glory of the Atonement.* Wheaton, Il: Crossway, 2007.

Pink, Arthur W., *The Atonement.* Swengel, PA: Reiner Publications.

_____, *Gleanings in Genesis.* Chicago, IL: Moody Press, 1975.

Schaeffer, Francis A., *How Shall We Then Live? The Rise and Decline of Western Thought and Culture.* Old Tappan, NJ: Fleming H. Revell Company, 1976.

Smeaton, George, *The Doctrine of the Atonement, as Taught by the Apostles.* Edinburgh: T&T Clark, 1870.

Smedes, Lewis B., *Can It Be All Right When Everything Is Wrong?* Wheaton, Il: Harold Shaw Publishing, 1999.

Stedman, Ray C., *Hebrews,* The IVP New Testament Commentary Series. Westmont, IL: IVP Academic, 1992.

Storms, Sam, *Christian Ethics*. Oklahoma City, OK: Sam Storms, 2006.

Stott, John R. W. *The Cross of Christ*. Leicester: Downers Grove, IL: IVP Books, 2006.

Studebaker, Steven M., *The Spirit of Atonement: Pentecostal Contributions and Challenges to the Christian Traditions*, ed. Daniela C. Augustine and Wolfgang Vondey, T&T Clark

Systematic Pentecostal and Charismatic Theology. London; New York; Oxford; New Delhi; Sydney: T&T Clark, 2021.

Swanson, James, *Dictionary of Biblical Languages with Semantic Domains: Hebrew (Old Testament)*. Oak Harbor: Logos Research Systems, Inc., 1997.

Synan, Vinson, *The Century of the Holy Spirit: 100 Years of Pentecostal and Charismatic Renewal*. Nashville, TE: Thomas Nelson Publishers, 2001.

Treat, Jeremy R., *The Crucified King; Atonement and Kingdom in Biblical and Systematic Theology*. Grand Rapids, MI: Zondervan, 2014.

Tozer, A. W. *The Radical Cross: Living the Passion of Christ*. Camp Hill, PA: WingSpread, 2005.

Walton, John H., *Genesis: The NIV Application Commentary*. Grand Rapids, MI: Zondervan, 2001

_____. *The Lost World of Adam and Eve*. Downers Grove, IL: InterVarsity Press, 2015.

Whitcomb, John C., Jr. and Henry M. Morris, *The Genesis Flood: The Biblical Record and Its Scientific Implications*. Philadelphia, PA: The Presbyterian and Reformed Publishing Co., 1974,

Williams, J. Rodman, *Renewal Theology: Systematic Theology from a Charismatic Perspective*, three volumes in one., Grand Rapids, MI: Zondervan, 1996.

Witherington III, Ben, *Biblical Theology: The Convergence of the Cannon.* Cambridge, United Kingdom: Cambridge University Press, 2019.

Zodhiates, Spiros, *The Complete Word Study Dictionary: New Testament.* Chattanooga, TN: AMG Publishers, 2000.

Sin: is
Self Centered, Willfull, Independent
from God.

Covenant: Gods Solemen binding
Committment between him self &
Other person & in an enter
Personal relationship to fullfill
Certain promises & Obligation &
                    ^ Purposes
thus providing the means of
security for all parties of the
Covenmment

God's contract is for life
Covenant sets boundaries
God only works thru a covenant
   Covenant's are consentinal

Mark 1:14-15
John 18:36
Rev 17:35
Romans 13:1-5
MARK 14:61-62
Matt 28:18-20
Rev
1 cor. 2 4-8
Eph 3:8-12
Col. 2:13-15
Eph 6:11-13
2 Thes. 2:8-12
Gal 6:14-16

Printed in the USA
CPSIA information can be obtained
at www.ICGtesting.com
CBHW070922070424
6447CB00003B/10